JOYCE & PARIS

1902.....1920 – 1940.....1975

Cover model produced by Industrie Service
Illustration André Masson

JOYCE & PARIS

1902.....1920 – 1940.....1975

PAPERS FROM THE FIFH INTERNATIONAL
JAMES JOYCE SYMPOSIUM

Paris 16-20 June 1975

edited by J. Aubert and M. Jolas

Editions du C.N.R.S.
15, quai Anatole-France
75700 PARIS

Publications de l'Université de Lille 3
B.P. 18
59650 VILLENEUVE-D'ASCQ

1979

© Publications de l'Université de Lille III / CNRS, 1979
ISBN 2-85939-106-1
ISBN 2-222-02389-0

Acknowledgements

The fifth " James Joyce International Symposium ", organized by the " James Joyce Foundation " (University of Tulsa, Oklahoma) under its then President, Bernard Benstock, in conjunction with the *Association Patrimoine Historique et Artistique de la France,* took place in Paris, from June 16 to June 20, 1975. It was sponsored by the French Government's *Secrétariat d'État à la Culture* and *Secrétariat aux Universités,* the British Council and the Cultural Services of the Irish Republic's Embassy in Paris. Essential material support was furnished by the *Centre National de la Recherche Scientifique.*

The *Centre National d'Art et de Culture Georges Pompidou* kindly offered the hospitality of one of its annexes in process of renovation, which also housed the exhibit entitled " James Joyce et Paris ", organized and presented by Bernard Gheerbrant under the auspices of the official *Bibliothèque Publique d'Information.* We wish to thank these authorities and these institutions whose co-operation was all the more appreciated in view of the fact that the Symposium coincided in time with a number of important French administrative changes. We take this opportunity to express our sincere regrets to any Symposium participants who may have been inconvenienced as a result of this situation.

Finally, we recall with gratitude the various indispensable services rendered both during the Symposium and while it was in preparation by : Mesdames P. Abravanel and Kathleen Bernard, Mademoiselle C. Chauvière and Monsieur J.F. Feige.

Kathleen Bernard's intelligent assistance in preparing this volume was invaluable.

Jacques AUBERT, Maria JOLAS, Fritz SENN

NOTICE

Presentation in printed form of the different working groups has been left to the judgement of those who presided. In some cases this has resulted in a synthesis furnished by the president, in others, in a series of individual papers, the minutes of a round-table or whatever form of discussion was chosen. Occasionally, it has not been possible to obtain a publishable text, in which case we have been limited to giving the title of the subject under consideration, the name of the person who presided and those of the participants who had been expected to attend. In general, it has been our aim to furnish those who were not present the maximum amount of information concerning the questions raised, as also the names of persons specializing in these questions, should it be desired to enter into contact with them.

The publisher has requested that the texts be grouped in two linguistic sections, according to the language that dominated the discussions. Our presentation follows the order and the calendar of the Symposium program.

" I write ", said JOYCE *

On February 23, 1934, thanks to the devoted and intelligent efforts of the well-known de luxe printer of rare books, François Bernouard, a group organized and presided by him, calling itself by the at once evocative and enigmatic name : " Les amis de 1914 ", introduced James Joyce and his " work in progress " to a wider Parisian public than they had known thus far. This event took place on the Boulevard Montparnasse, in a vast temporary wooden structure, next door to *La Coupole,* which had opened its enormous, still popular tavern, in 1927. And when the *Nouvelles Littéraires* reported the affair, the article was headlined : « Joyce à la Coupole. ».

That evening Joyce was in particularly congenial company : on the stage were Louis Gillet, Léon-Paul Fargue and Edouard Dujardin, all three of whom defended the work with eloquence and conviction ; while in the audience, there were his many friends of that period, whose names I take pleasure in recalling : André Spire, Sylvia Beach, Adrienne Monnier, Ludmila Bloch-Savitsky, Mr. and Mrs. John Rodker, Mr. and Mrs. Stuart Gilbert, Helen and Georgio Joyce, the Paul Léons, the Myron Nuttings, the John O'Sullivans, Robert McAlmon, Samuel Beckett, George Antheil, Philippe Soupault... and if Ezra Pound or Valery Larbaud, Lawrence and Kay Boyle Vail, James and Tania Stern, the Desmond Harmsworths − the list might well have been longer − had happened to be in Paris on that evening, no doubt they too would have been present. For we had all rallied round, and the large hall, il I remember rightly, was filled.

Throughout the evening, the author himself remained silent. I do not think,however, that this was to be attributed to his famous motto. For he was happy that a talented French actress, Rachel Behrendt, who was perfectly bilingual, should have agreed to read aloud a fragment from *Finnegans Wake.* He had coached her over the rough spots and, actually, in addition to her perfect pronunciation of the English words, one sensed that she had understood the subtler coloration of the language of the *Wake* which, as we know, is a language that casts a spell of its own. In an important essay entitled " Joyce and the Present

---

* Opening session, Grand Amphithéâtre de la Sorbonne.

Age ", written in honour of Joyce's 50th birthday, the Viennese author-critic Hermann Broch, has lent a rarely sensitive ear to this language. Here is the passage :

> " ... Two washerwomen are kneeling on the bank of the river, washing dirty clothes. Across the water they are exchanging bits of gossip about the town and about the heroine, Anna Livia Plurabelle. Their conversation continues to the rhythm of their washing, with its rubbing and beating. In fact, their conversation is itself washing, for the reason that they are washing the dirty linen of the whole town. But as darkness falls and the mist lowers, the conversation lags and the movements of the washerwomen slacken ; the river grows wider and wider in the deepening mist, its murmur becomes more and more audible. The murmur of the river intrudes upon the conversation, for nothing is described, everything originates in and out of the talk of the washerwomen who have now ceased to be washerwomen, but have become fabulous beings, one the stem of a shrub on the bank, the other a piece of stone, both lapped by the swelling waves, and their talk finally nothing but the dying murmur of the river, incomprehensible to the listener, incomprehensible to themselves, music of the water, embodied in human sound, which is scarcely speech any longer. And if I may make a personal confession, I find it indescribably beautiful... " [1]

The evening having passed off well, Joyce decided to suggest to the British Broadcasting Corporation, which thus far had remained aloof to his new work, a programme based on Rachel Behrendt's reading. The plan seemed to be all the more possible of acceptance since Sir Harley Granville-Barker, whose influence on the B.B.C.'s choice of artists was preponderant, was visiting Paris at the time. Joyce asked me to act as his messenger on this occasion, which I did. I was disappointed to have to report a categorical refusal.

Finnegans Wake was published in London in May 1939. It left British readers more or less indifferent due in part, we may suppose, to their comprehensible concern over the threat of war. " War will come ", Joyce had said to me when the book was due to appear, " and nobody will read it ".

Ulysses, we recall, appeared in 1922, and Joyce died in 1941. As late as 1948, however, the authoritative " Times Literary Supplement " published an unsigned article that described *Ulysses* as " a literary oddity by a gifted writer " adding " it is hard to see how it can ever or ever could be otherwise regarded ". The article continued : " However, Tristram Shandy is also a literary oddity, and it has lasted close on a couple of hundred years to date. For *Finnegans Wake* we feel inclined to offer no such hope ".

If Joyce received practically no official honours during his lifetime, they have also been slow in coming since his death. In spite of his universal fame, there still remain important pockets of indifference and ignorance. It is for this reason

---

(1) English translation from a mimeograph script, by E. and M. Jolas, in " A Joyce Yearbook ", Transition Press, Paris 1949. Original German text in " Dichten und Erkennen ", Rhein Verlag, Zurich 1955. French translation by Albert Kohn in " Création littéraire et connaissance ", Gallimard, Paris 1966.

that after Dublin and Trieste, today's ceremony in this city where he chose to live and work for 20 years, in these prestigious surroundings, and under these auspices, is for us who are delegates to this Fifth Symposium, as also for the old friends and collaborators of Joyce gathered here today, a source of deep satisfaction. It gives me great pleasure to express in my own name, in that of those who were closest to Joyce, and in the name of readers everywhere for whom, to quote T.S. Eliot, this great œuvre « forms a whole ", our warm appreciation. I even dare to hope that tomorrow, or some day soon, we shall have the pleasure of reading in the French press an article which, echoing the article of 1934, will be headlined " Joyce à la Sorbonne ".

Before introducing my friend, Doctor Jacques Lacan, I should like to recall an incident that, for me, is typical of the man, James Joyce.

I was invited to accompany him to a reception organized by the " British Institute " in Paris in honour of the author of *The Golden Bough,* Sir James Frazer. The room was very crowded and with many other late arrivals, we formed in line to be presented to the guest of honour. Finally, it was Joyce's turn to be introduced :

" What name ? " Frazer asked him.

" Joyce, James Joyce ", was the reply.

" And what do you do ? " Sir James questioned politely.

" I write ", said Joyce.

We moved on, and were soon lost in the crowd.

Maria JOLAS

" *Circe* " :
why, what and how

Circe and the epiphany concept

The " oft discussed and much maligned " topic of epiphanies is all too familiar to scholars and serious readers of the works of James Joyce. The question of the validity of epiphanies and even the epiphany concept itself are still subject to serious debate among Joyce scholars. The popular definition of the term as it is used in most Joyce classes is that it represents a revelation of truth to the protagonist or reader. The question now has shifted to whether the epiphany constitutes a genuine revelation of truth of character or situation, or whether it only has the appearance of truth to the consciousness which perceives it. In the familiar equation of epiphanies with post-Aristotelian recognitions, the protagonist discovers a truth about his character, so that historically the epiphany concept has become linked with the tragic flaw and the acquisition of self-knowledge in tragedies and novels.

The development of the epiphany into the creation of a work of art within the story or novel itself has its roots at least as far back as the aesthetic movement in the late nineteenth century, and extends into a substantial number of works in modern and contemporary literature. The idea is that the artist in recreating or reordering the events of his life into a meaningful pattern creates not only a work of art but an order for his own existence. Whether there is more truth to the art than the every day dross from which it is made is, however, doubtful at best. That experience purified as artistic creation assumes eternal validity, is even more suspect when we realize that nearly all self-perceptions follow this same process. I would, however, hesitate to state categorically that every one of my own self-perceptions is likely to be any more truthful than anyone else's perception of me. The point is that like any self-perceptions, the perceptions of the characters in Joyce's works, their epiphanies, may in fact be totally false, and even though transformed by the characters' artistic creativity, they may be no more than self-delusions.

This is most apparent in the book of many epiphanies, *Dubliners*. To cite only two examples, Mr. Duffy's epiphany of loneliness is based in part upon his conviction that Mrs. Sinico turned to drink and eventual self-destruction because he broke off their relationship. When we take into account the fact that Mrs. Sinico did not begin her drinking until two years after her estrangement from Duffy that assumption is certainly questionable. Asexual Duffy's last compelling vision of the phallic train creeping along laboriously with the fiery head is triggered by furtive lovers engaged in affairs in which he can take no part. Duffy has, after all, received little more than a pat on the cheek from the enamored Sinico. When his recurrent metaphor of being a stranger at love's feast has its roots in the cold grease on his dinner plate, one must ask how much validity his epiphany holds.

The final and perhaps most moving epiphany of *Dubliners* is experienced by Gabriel Conroy who is, of course, an artist. His vision of himself as a ludicrous figure and his epiphany of the Christ-like Furey with thorns and crooked crosses is his final revelation. Each of the three prominent women in the story reduces Gabriel to an insight of self-degradation : Lily on the stairs, Miss Ivors in the upper chambers, and Bertha in the Gresham Hotel. Each time Gabriel suffers, seeing himself a ludicrous figure, and each time he manages to pull himself together and rise to new heights. The last epiphany, however, with its overripe, purple prose is Gabriel's strongest revelation of his own ludicrousness, of his ineffectuality and inability to create the lasting truth that the consumptive Furey has in his death. But the epiphany is of course Gabriel's. He has manufactured the image of Furey from the scant details Gretta has provided him. Gabriel has framed the image of the snow all over Ireland uniting the living and dead and he has made the great leap from his own epiphany to the much wider perspective of the meaning of life not only in his own situation but in Ireland generally. Gabriel's image of his own ineffectuality gives credence to the strong final image which, because Gabriel creates it, belies his ineffectuality at the same time it asserts it. It does not come to Gabriel out of the blue but has been psychologically prepared for by all of the things that have happened to him earlier in the story. It represents the artistically arranged, cumulative effect of the events of his consciousness, no more or less.

Much the same is true of Stephen Dedalus' great epiphany on the beach in Chapter 4 of *A Portrait of the Artist as a Young Man*. His image of the woman clothed in the garb of a bird is a compilation of all the female and bird images that have preceded, and the metaphor is framed in the words and language which we have seen Stephen use through the rest of *Portrait*. The image is essentially an artistic recreation of all of the psychological and historical forces that have come into play in Stephen's consciousness, as well as such external things as the drops of water in the brimming bowl, the bog water in the ditch and a host of other artifacts of his experience.

In his aesthetic theory Stephen tries to rationalize the epiphany relationship to the goal of artistry in his life. There the artist sees his own image in immediate relationship to himself and to others. In order to be an artist of the highest art, the poet presents the self-generated epiphanies of his own life with the objectivity of a playwright standing behind the scenes paring his fingernails, refining and transforming his perceptions and misperceptions into abstractions of art. Since self-knowledge and perceptions are not limited to artists, it follows that the artist has no more validity in his epiphany, which is presented in the form of a work of art derived from his own experiences and filtered through his own consciousness, than have any of the rest of us erring mortals who may be wrong or right. In the sense that we all have these perceptions we are all artists. Hence the images of Bloom and Stephen in *Ulysses*.

Obviously Bloom's confrontation with Gerty McDowell on the beach in Nausicaa is a commentary on its parallel scene in Chapter 4 of *Portrait*. The thoughts of Bloom and Gerty are in fact a mundane replica of Stephen's earlier artistic triumph. It has been noted elsewhere that Bloom and Stephen go through similar experiences all through *Ulysses,* creating in effect a sense of identification between the two. Hence in Circe their respective illusions are the product often of each other's experiences during the day. Like the other revelations of Joyce's characters, the epiphanies of Circe, which stem from the conscious and subconscious minds of Stephen and Bloom, have all been manufactured from the experiences the two have undergone on June 16, and are framed in the thoughts and language which they have been sharing through the day. Like Conroy and the characters of *Dubliners,* as well as Stephen in *Portrait,* their epiphanies culminate in an illusion of self-knowledge, but this time with a difference : the form is a parody of art and Stephen's aesthetic theory ; it is a drama where the epiphany is presented in immediate relation to others. Their realizations of their own inadequacies, their debasements and their aggrandizements culminate for Bloom in the snapping of his trousers' button, and Stephen's Siegfried-like breaking of the hold of the old gods by smashing the chandelier with his ashplant-sword. Joyce is presenting the same epiphany approach that he has in his other books, only this time in comic form, as he explores the epiphany-making process as well as the nature of the epiphany itself. Those things which have registered themselves in the two protagonists' subconsciousness come back in rarified artistic form in Circe, transformed into works of art, but with little more validity than have the original experiences or the recognitions of the other epiphany beholders in Joyce's works. Stephen's Siegfried emerges as cuckolded, like his Shakespearean counterpart, Bloom, and with so much in common that Stephen identifies with the mundane man he has just met : " I am twentytwo too. Sixteen years ago I twentytwo tumbled, twentytwo years ago he sixteen fell off his hobby-horse. "(*U*563)

But Stephen has no more ability to communicate than he had before. Even in a simple conversation in the street Stephen is virtually unable to pass the time of day with Cissy Caffrey and her two escorts. Stephen does, however, see the similarity between himself and Bloom, although he is not freed in the traditional self-recognition sense of Aristotelean tragedy by his epiphany. His trouble with his mother is not behind him. His artistry or his ability to communicate it is no better than it ever was. Bloom on the other hand thinks he has found a son but hasn't.

The only art in which Stephen's discovery results is the phantom Professor McGinty's dance of death. Perhaps the ultimate realization that Bloom and Stephen are somehow related will someday enable the young writer to go on to write *Ulysses,* but by the end of Circe, that is only the wildest sort of extrapolation. In this epiphany chapter of Joyces's epiphanies, the final image of Stephen as a little Rudy provides the ultimate comic vision. Though Joyce's is indeed a world of the imagination, it is a world in which he makes no claims for any understanding of ultimate reality.

Zack BOWEN
University of Delaware

A note or two on form and content in " CIRCE "

More than anything else in the Joyce canon, " Circe " is a *trip,* a hallucinogenic trip. And as in all trips − whether the getting from point "A" to point "X" is external and physical or internal and metaphysical or any combination thereof − incidents occur which produce changes in the people involved, and influence or determine their subsequent actions.

In this Joycean trip we find, as James Carens observed earlier, just about everything that we find in *Ulysses* itself : every motif, every concept, every mood, every device. There was never anything quite like " Circe " before ; there has never been anything quite like it since : masque, extravaganza, three-ring circus, sociological document, penetrating character study, vaudeville, slapstick, farce, black humor, the Absurd.

" Circe " is an enormous surrealistic prose poem. In spite of its great length, its huge cast of characters, its enormous range of mood and tone, and its manic activity, the episode seems to me to be structurally without flaws. Some of the earlier episodes of *Ulysses* occasionally become enmired in technique ("Aeolus" and "Sirens", for example) ; even the best of the later episodes have their awkward, heavy, repetitious, or soggy moments ; but in "Circe" there are no false moves, no wasted moments, no unnecessary words : all parts contribute to an unparalelled whole.

Efforts to translate " Circe " into other media thus far have for the most part been unsuccessful. To be effectively transfigured, all contemporary art-and-entertainment genres as varied as " Circe " itself must be melded : dance, music, traditional and experimental visual art (above all else, COLOR, without which " Circe " is as unthinkable as, say, Chagall's *Arabische Nächte* paintings would be in black and white), and finally, of course, every known cinematic technique. Only film can eventually capture " Circe ".

Paradoxically, " Circe ", the most ambitious, experimental, and technically daring episode in *Ulysses,* expresses perhaps Joyce's most conventional and traditional concepts : when robbed of his reason, man can sink lower than the lowest beast ; contemporary urban society is sick, sick, sick ; individual man, deprived of love and understanding, becomes lost in an alien or hostile desert, swallowed up in a nightmare of meaningless activity, imprisoned in a room with no exit. But in spite of this, the dominant mood of " Circe " is one of gusto, of affirmation, not death or decay. " Circe " is Chaucerian, not Dantean or Homeric (and is even occasionally illuminated with a remarkable sense of *gentleness,* the kind of gentleness that those who knew Joyce well have occasionally recorded in their reminiscences... I am thinking here particularly of some of Kay Boyle and Robert McAlmon's recollections in *Being Geniuses Together).*

Nowhere in Joyce does form suggest or reenforce meaning more effectively than in " Circe " and nowhere in Joyce – including " Sirens " – do music parallels play a more significant role. Consider the apparition of Rudy at the close of the episode, a tranquil figure in a moment of calm after the chaos and frenzied activity of the episode as a whole, with its grossness, obscenity, absurdity, burlesque, the grotesque, the surreal, and the ridiculous :

> ...a fairy boy of eleven, a changeling... in an Eton suit... holding a book in his hand... He reads from right to left inaudibly, smiling, kissing the page... Gazes unseeing into Bloom's face and goes on reading, kissing, smiling...

A moment of complete *silence* in which the crowded stage is suddenly emptied and cleansed. An eternity of ineffable calm and tranquillity comparable to the calm and tranquillity of the adagio of the third movement in Beethoven's Ninth Symphony. A voiceless eternity, a complete *withdrawal*. It is a truism that the spiritual peace of the third movement, following as it does the intense activity and threatened disaster of the first and second movements, is evoked by a series of variations with little or no forward movement, a search for release from fate and destiny in which *nothing actually happens*. Such a quest for withdrawal, such attainment of peaceful self-contemplation, is essentially Oriental and brings us once again to Bloom's yearning for the East : though the moment of tranquillity will soon end it *has* been attained, though perhaps without Bloom or Stephen's awareness. Joyce, once again and never with greater quiet grandeur, has transmuted a mass of incidents into myth.

So the trip ends, back where it began ?

No, not quite. I tend to agree with Zack Bowen's comment that in effect " nothing really happens " to Stephen and Bloom in " Circe ". *In " Circe ", perhaps not. But afterwards,* yes, depending upon how each individual reader interprets the remaining episodes of the myth, remembering finally, that " Circe ", like *Ulysses,* is cyclical rather than linear, and :

If the episode ends where it began, at midnight, with Bloom and Stephen apart, in the Mabbott Street entrance of Nighttown, it ends with them together, in the pre-dawn.

William PEDEN
University of Missouri.

Gesture in "Circe"

The style of "Circe" depends on modes of gesture : people, stage props, and visions act and speak, converting inner realities into external movements or gestures. The psychological and mental processes of the protagonists become external, acted out in a series of gestures. That mode of expression makes the chapter a clearer — in part because a more overt and less censored — exploration of Stephen's and Bloom's minds. Thus gesture becomes a method of communication, a method possible only within the dramatic form of the chapter, and a method that allows us as readers to understand more fully the characters — that is, gesture is a more universal language than words. The non-English speaker would understand Bloom's latent masochism, for instance, without understanding words if he could *see* that psychological quirk manifest on the " stage ". Stephen points to the significance of gesture on the fourth page of the chapter : " So that gesture, not music, not odours, would be a universal language, the gift of tongues rendering visible not the lay sense but the first entelechy, the structural rhythm " (*U,* 432). That gesture renders " structural rhythm " " visible ", associates it with time, for both rhythm and the visible exist within time. That Stephen wishes to associate gesture with eternity, to remove it from time, hints at one of his problems with gesture, hence with communication at the essential level, and with his art. Within time, communication with other human beings is possible because people exist within time ; dissociated from time, Stephen can communicate with himself, with God, or with the dead, but he cannot communicate with people.

"Circe" itself moves out of linear and regular time into a time that is uneven, halting, jerky. Like the characters' minds this time is unshared and unsharable ; Bloom cannot share his psychological traumas with Stephen, Stephen cannot share his with Bloom. The stage directions and the actions of the characters and props mimic the irregularity of time. A " *deafmute idiot ... jerks past* " (429), " *A crone ... heaves his booty, tugs askew his peaked cap and hobbles off mutely* ", " *A drunken navvy ...* [is] *lurching heavily* ", the soldiers " *march unsteadily* " (430) : none moves rhythmically, in a normal relationship to time. Their gestures appear abnormal, or distorted, or sick, or drunken ; the gestures of the protagonists, when removed from shared time, appear abnormal, sick, distorted or drunken. Stephen's comments and the stage directions, then, alert us to the thematic significance of gesture and time.

There are, it seems to me, two different kinds of gestures : the kind Stephen is interested in — personal, eternal, private — the kind of gesture that we see when Simon swoops down on Stephen-fox. And there is the second gesture, the external and shared. Stephen's internal gestures clearly communicate to us ; they are, however, not controlled by him, not shaped by the young artist. They are, moreover, in conflict with his art. To demonstrate gesture at all he first must relinquish his ashplant, the symbol or talisman of his art : although he is positing gesture as the primary mode of art, in order to communicate a gesture to Lynch, he must give up that sense of art that is manifested in his ashplant.

> This movement illustrates the loaf and jug of bread and wine in Omar. Hold my stick.
>
> . . . .
>
> *(Stephen thrusts the ashplant on him and slowly holds out his hands...)* (433).

One gesture, the demonstration of gesture, is dependent upon another gesture, the relinquishing of art-ashplant. I asked myself why. If the finest art is gesture, why would Stephen have to reject his art to adopt gesture ?

The answer to that question, perhaps, lies in the nature of Stephen's art. Tracing the ashplant through " Circe ", we discover that the dance with the whores, a series of patterned gestures, ends for Stephen as he reverts to his ashplant :

> *(He wheels Kitty into Lynch's arms, snatches up his ashplant from the table and takes the floor... Stephen with hat ashplant frogsplits in middle highkicks with skykicking mouth clasp part under thigh...)* (578).

Once again shared gesture is incompatible with the ashplant. As Stephen dances with his onanistic symbol, he rejects the external and shared sense of gesture. Dance patterns a series of actions, or gestures, and implies relationships among people ; Stephen can only accept relationships with his private, unshared art, that is, with himself. He is, thus, an unsuccessful artist (he cannot communicate even through that primary language), and an unsuccessful human being (his actions and gestures elicit nothing but terror from the whores, pity and charity from Leopold).

Not only does Stephen reject the universal nature of gesture, he also rejects the regular time implied in the word rhythmic. In " Circe ", Stephen denies time and normalcy as he smashes the chandelier with the ashplant (art) and attempts to create " *Time's livid final flame* " (583), or to end time. But his effort is not successful. While the inspiration for this gesture, as for all others, may well be purely internal and private, the gesture itself is an outer and public act, occurring within time. Bella's response, a demand for ten shillings, insists on the reality of gesture within the mundane world.

The implications of Stephen's acts for his art are devastating. Gesture in " Circe " stands in the same relationship to psychology as word does to literary shaping. Both are the outward manifestations of inner qualities, both make the " universal ", or the thing " known to all men " out of the esoteric, both are shaped and patterned by conscious and unconscious means. As Stephen struggles for the " word known to all men ", he struggles for gesture. And he ends the chapter − as in fact he begins it − partly paralyzed, unable to act, or gesture. The ashplant − his masturbatory and esoteric art − prevents communication or manifestation ; it prevents real shaping, real art.

Bloom, in contrast, refuses to deny time. When his own attraction to the eternal and private becomes a gesture, manifested in the nymph's appeal, he rejects her. In his public and communal gestures he does not deny time, nor commit any indecipherable acts. Although the time sequences controlled by Bloom's mind-psyche appear in the novel to be as irregular, and hence to accommodate gestures whose rhythms and meanings are as irregular or unshared as Stephen's, we know that Bloom's external gestures are patterned and regular, and that they allow the whores to understand him. If they did not, the women would clue us to some disparity between Bloom's acts and their expectations. At the end of the chapter, while Stephen mutters and lies unable to move, Bloom's acts, his gestures, if not his mind, focus upon Stephen, not the dead Rudy. He moves back into linear and shared time.

Joyce appears to be indicating both that the real truth, if it exists, exists in men's minds, that psychological life is more real than physical life, and at the same time that moral truth and success in art or life exist, if at all, in men's actions. Men should be judged on the series of gestures they make, on how well their gestures communicate themselves and shape the chaos inside them and outside them. Psychological-spiritual life is internal, unique and without any sense of accountability ; external and shared life is communal, responsible, accountable. One's success is measured by how closely the two lives match, or harmonize, or by whether external gesture, the word known to all men and the universal language, does communicate an individual man's being. By those standards, Bloom is successful with gesture and analogously with words ; Stephen is not. Bloom shapes and patterns successfully, Stephen does not. Bloom, rather than Stephen, achieves an artistry that is at once personally true and shared.

Marguerite HARKNESS
Virginia Commonwealth University

Social significances
of Bloom's psychology in " Circe "

When Stephen Dedalus, in the " Circe " episode of *Ulysses,* says, " The harlot's cry from street to street/ Shall weave old Ireland's windingsheet ", he means by this pretty much what Blake meant when he said, " The harlot's cry from street to street/ Shall weave old England's winding sheet " : that the fate or doom of a nation where" souls of men are bought and sold/ and beauty for a bit of gold " will hang on this transaction because the underside of life reflects the underside of people's souls. In " Circe " Joyce uses prostitution as a symbol for modern civilization in its commercial, capitalistic materialism.

In doing so, he prefigures such later works as Norman Mailer's *The Deer Park* (1955), which equates prostitution with Hollywood and Hollywood with America, and Jean-Luc Godard's *Deux ou trois choses que je sais d'elle* (1966), in which a prostitute symbolizes France. Joyce's massive presentation of a world ruled by vice also looks backward to the late Medieval tradition that the material world is ruled by Satan. Thus, at one of the climaxes of " Circe ", both a Catholic priest and a Protestant clergyman preside over a black Mass, an apotheosis of the evil which God allows to hold sway.

The world ruled by a God equated with Satan in which Stephen and Leopold Bloom find themselves is a world of dispossession. Stephen's mother has been taken from him by God, while Bloom's wife has been taken from him by the Satanic Blazes Boylan. Both men are constantly preoccupied by thoughts of the women they have lost. The principle that the virtuous man cannot unite with or possess physical beauty, a principle which makes prostitution inevitable, is embodied on the political level in *Ulysses* by the theme of spiritual nations enslaved by material ones. In " Nestor ", " Aeolus " and alsewhere, the Greeks, Jews and Irish are identified as sensitive peoples fated by history to lie under the yokes of the crude materialist empires of Egypt, Britain and Rome, both pagan and Vatican.

On the personal level, the state of dispossession in which the sensitive person finds himself corresponds to the œdipal complex and the son's realization that his mother has already given herself to his father. If he cannot overcome this dispossession by associating with the father because he has, say, a weak, irresponsible father like Stephen's or a dead one like Bloom's, he will remain fixated as a son and never be able to possess a woman without reference to a paternal other. Whether he hates and defies the inevitable competitor, as Stephen does, or almost realizes that he needs another man, as Bloom does, he is incapable of possessing the world as an independent man. As Norman O. Brown has pointed out, the œdipal complex has much the same effect as the idea of original sin : it tells us we are guilty and in need of authority because of something in the dim past we do not remember doing.

Joyce's ideology was disturbed by the injustice involved in making the son, who was closer to spirit, a servant of the father sunken into matter. If sensitivity is life, then the Irish, Greeks and Jews are more alive than those they serve, and this state of affairs supports portrayal of the world as scortatory.

The word *mother* is cognate with *matter* as Molly is equated with earth, and the inconstant mother is also mutability. Thus, the three whores Kitty, Floey and Zoe, as animal, vegetable and mineral, cover the phenomenal world. Everywhere Stephen looks he sees time eating matter, father violating mother, God kissing her with death : " He comes, pale vampire... mouth to her mouth's kiss ". Similarly, Bloom has constantly to tell himself not to think of Blazes and Molly and his own need for a surrogate father. And because he knows the hour of assignation, Bloom thinks of time passing whenever he thinks of Boylan ; so that Boylan for Bloom, like God for Stephen, plays the essential paternal role of enforcer of passing time. Just as Stephen hears a clock in heaven strike eleven, Bloom hears Boylan " sonnez la cloche ".

As the underside of life emerges in " Circe ", the characters confront the realities behind the society they live in and the underlying forces in their own minds. Nothing that happens differs essentially from what was going on all day, but patterns which were under the surface earlier appear here in extreme and explicit forms. The major drives in Bloom's life center on material involvement, at the expense of his own identity, in a world which is passing him by, and on attraction to inanimate objects. These drives correspond to the sexual activities of masochism, cuckoldry and coprophilia.

The two major fantasies Bloom has in " Circe " feature long scenes in which he is abused by aggressive women. In the first he is flagellated by Mrs. Yelverton Barry, Mrs. Bellingham and the Honourable Mrs. Mervyn Talboys ; in the second, he is ridden by Bella Cohen. Bloom has shown an attraction to " weightcarrying huntresses " all day from " Calypso ", when he imagined the servant girl in the butcher shop beating her carpet ; and Molly in oriental garb abuses him early in " Circe ".

Bloom reacts to the social, psychological and philosophical position of dispossession by putting the blame on woman. In this way he avoids the hopeless conflict with paternal authority in which Stephen is locked, just as he avoids the thought of Boylan. If one must have authority, it is easier to submit to mother than father, and so Bloom elevates woman to the position of deity. His god is personified as natural phenomenon in " Oxen of the Sun " : " ... he saw that he was in the land of Phenomenon where he must for a certain, one day die... ".Whenever he is confronted with images of violence or threat, he invokes natural phenomenon to protect him. In " Cyclops ", for example, when he hears talk of ejaculation during hanging, he says, " That can be explained by science... It's only a natural phenomenon... ". The nameless narrator of " Cyclops " is moved by his disgust at Bloom's amelioration by technique to exclaim, " Phenomenon ! The fat heap he married is a nice old phenomenon with a back on her like a ballalley ". And this is quite fitting, for Molly is the central embodiment of Bloom's God.

Bloom's maternal deity, however, is a disguise for ultimately male authority, as we see most obviously when Bella changes to Bello. His aggressive women are partly men in disguise, and both his masochistic fantasies are triggered by images of authority which represent paternal threats, though the fantasies concentrate on women.

Bloom's first trial begins when he sees two policemen pass. His anxiety about his position in society makes him imagine them using the accusative at him and as he has just fed a dog, they charge him with " prevention of cruelty to animals " (p. 454). Hereupon Signor Maffei, a character from *Ruby : The Pride of the Ring,* describes sadistic techniques for training animals, " even *Leo ferox* there ", and introduces " Mademoiselle Ruby, the pride of the ring ". Maffei's methods exemplify the use of force by society to condition its citizens, and Bloom insists throughout this scene that he is loyal to the King. Reference to him as Ruby prefigures his later sex change with Bello and suggests that he reads sado-masochistic novels from the point of view of the victim.

The second scene begins after a creaking door handle causes Zoe to say, " The devil is in that door " (p. 525) and Bloom imagines that Blazes is outside, the aggressive male competitor who gets the plums. When Bella now enters, her first observation of Bloom is that he is married. Joyce implied from " A Little Cloud " that every husband is potentially a cuckold to every bachelor because the married man has bound himself to socially sanctioned use of one woman while the bachelor can circulate freely.

Bella is the aggressive type of the organizer or administrator, the kind of person who runs society. In his notesheets for " Circe ", Joyce wrote, " flatty (BC) ", implying that he thought of Bella in Irish slang as a police officer. Bello smokes a cigar, reads stock news in a business paper and speaks of friends who are officers and gentlemen. The clergy also joins the abuse of Bloom in that two priests present him with a cuckoo clock during his first ordeal while the Nymph, who presents him with the ultimate temptation to debasement after Bello, finally appears in a nun's habit. Thus, all of the forces of the social order, the aristocracy, business, the state, the Church and sheer physical aggressiveness unite to degrade Bloom's fantasy self in " Circe " as they unite to degrade his unconscious mind during the daylight hours when he is not aware of these fantasies.

Sheldon BRIVIC
Temple University

Non-Dramatic Illusion in "Circe"

We customarily speak of the "Circe" episode of *Ulysses* as a drama of one sort or another. Richard Kain, for instance, describes the Nighttown sequence as a dramatization of the subconscious, "the night-side of the mind" (1); in this episode, Kain says, "the hidden fears and desires [of Stephen and Bloom] become dramatized, as in dreams" (2). Harry Blamires believes that "What happens in the mind is expressed in dramatic form exactly as what happens externally is expressed" (3), and more recently David Hayman has spoken of hallucinations in "Circe", arguing that Joyce "plunges us into not one but two overwrought psyches artfully interrelated" (4). Even Joyce himself seems to support the view that "Circe" is a drama of the mind, since he described the technique of the chapter as "hallucination" (5).

My contention is simple. I believe that Stephen and Bloom are not literally undergoing hallucinations, that the term "hallucination" applies primarily to the technique rather than to the content of "Circe", and that the episode is actually a narrative, not a drama.

Perhaps my point will be clearer if we digress for a moment to that part of the "Sirens" chapter where Miss Kennedy and Miss Douce are discussing "that old fogey in Boyd's" while Bloom walks along Wellington Quay toward Essex Bridge (pp. 259-260) (6). The barmaids have a great deal of fun talking about the pharmacist, with his "goggle eye" and "bit of beard" and "greasy nose"; and as they choke and cough and giggle over the notion of "being married to a man like that" — "Married to the greasy nose!" — the narrator steps well outside of the realistic framework of the episode, deliberately confuses the pharmacist with Bloom, and snickers, "Married to Bloom, to greaseaseabloom". Clearly, Misses Douce and Kennedy have *not* been discussing Bloom, who at 38 is hardly an "old fogey" and who in any case has no beard (7), yet Blamires inexplicably maintains

(1) Richard Kain, *Fabulous Voyager* (1947; rpt. New York: Compass, 1967), p. 137.
(2) Kain, p. 31.
(3) Harry Blamires, *The Bloomsday Book* (London: Methuen, 1966), p. 166.
(4) David Hayman, *Ulysses: The Mechanics of Meaning* (Englewood Cliffs, N.J.: Prentice-Hall, 1970), p. 32.
(5) See the schema reproduced in Stuart Gilbert, *James Joyce's Ulysses* (1930; rpt. New York: Vintage, 1952), p. 30. In the Linati schema the technique of "Circe" is more accurately described as "Vision animated to bursting-point"; see Richard Ellmann, *Ulysses on the Liffey* (New York: Oxford University Press, 1973), Appendix.
(6) *Ulysses* (New York: Modern Library, 1961). All references are to this edition.
(7) See Joyce's caricature of Bloom, reproduced by Richard Ellman in *James Joyce* (New York: Oxford University Press, 1959), facing P. 433. In this picture Bloom has a mustache but no beard.

that the girls have seen and are now talking about Bloom (8), and even such a perceptive critic as Franz Stanzel can say that " Miss Douce and Miss Kennedy have seen Bloom as he passes by the hotel and now giggle at the inconceivable prospect of marriage with this figure " (9). What actually happens is quite different : while the barmaids discuss the pharmacist, and Bloom (whom the girls may never have seen before) approaches the hotel, the narrator telescopes the two events, partly to underscore Bloom's sexual frustration. In deviating so sharply from the clearly defined level of realistic narration (not only here but elsewhere in " Sirens ") the narrator follows a pattern established earlier, in the parodies in " Scylla and Charybdis " (for instance, in the parody of the Apostle's Creed and in the mock-dramatic passage in which characters are named " Mageeglinjohn " and " Quakerlyster "). Like the headlines in " Aeolus " and the burlesque style of the non-realistic portions of " Cyclops ", the narrator's intrusion in " Sirens " is deliberately artificial ; and the more drastic the abandonment of realistic narration, the more we are aware of Joyce's artful manipulation of the action.

Yet like the magician he is, Joyce pulls his best trick while pretending to show all of his cards. The paradox of " Circe " is its apparent objectivity as a dramatic presentation, the illusion being that the reader seems to be moving back and forth between Bloom's and Stephen's inner worlds and an objectively verifiable outer world. Presumably, then, when Pat the waiter appears (p. 447) and says " Steak and kidney. Bottle of lager. Hee hee hee. Wait till I wait ", we are meant to think that Bloom is recalling his little joke about the " waiter who waits while you wait " (p. 280). Actually, though, there is little evidence that Bloom is literally thinking of Pat : for one thing, in the fantasy sequences in " Circe " Bloom sees several characters whom he encountered earlier in the day, but later on, when he might remember having had some sort of hallucination about these people, he doesn't. Even such memorable events as Bloom's rise to power and his trial make no impression on him, and for good reason : these are really the narrator's fantasies, not Bloom's (10).

The common notion that the episode actually represents Bloom's and Stephen's hallucinations in fairly straightforward fashion is surprising because all of Joyce's narrative devices are displayed quite openly. First, there are the stage directions, which remind us of the presence of a narrator by *narrating* events and thereby controlling our point of view. Furthermore, the chapter begins before either Stephen or Bloom arrives on the scene ; and if we assume that this early part of " Circe ", including the expressionistic representation of the whistles as disembodied characters named The Calls and The Answers, is the product of either Stephen's mind or Bloom's or both, then we must account for the absence of

---

(8) Blamires, p. 109. In his review of Blamires' book, Fritz Senn calls attention to this error (*JJQ*, 4 [Summer 1967], 348).

(9) Franz Stanzel, *Narrative Situations in the Novel,* trans. James P. Pusack (Bloomington : Indiana University Press, 1971), p. 127.

(10) Although I did not know it when I first presented this paper in Paris, Anthony Burgess takes a similar position in *Re Joyce* (New York : Norton, 1965), pp. 158-159.

the character whose visions are supposedly being dramatized. Moreover, the old complaint that in this chapter Stephen and Bloom know more than they could possibly know can be answered if we consider the possibility that they don't really know all of these things. But the narrator, the controller of the action – what Hayman calls the " arranger " (11) – does, just as the narrator of " Sirens " knows when Bloom is on his way to the Ormond Hotel.

The narrator does not know everything, though : even in reporting facts he is not entirely reliable, for he is capable of saying, for example, that Stephen " *chants with joy the* introit *for paschal time* " (p. 431), whereas what Stephen actually chants is " the Antiphon that is used with the Asperges during Paschaltide " (12). Moreover, the narrator of " Circe " is characterized by his fondness for word play : he describes Bloom's image in a concave mirror as " *lovelorn longlost lugubru Booloohoom* " (pp. 433-434) to imitate the mirror's distorting effects, and he imagines The Voice of All the Damned singing " Alleluia, for the Lord God Omnipotent reigneth ! " backwards in order to demonstrate comically the contest between divine and satanic forces (p. 599). Of course, the fantasies of " Circe " are not totally divorced from the consciousnesses of Stephen and Bloom ; they are narrational extrapolations from the characters' very real fears and desires, and they probably tell us as much about Stephen and Bloom as real hallucinations would. (In one sense they are rather like the parodic narrations in " Cyclops ", although the narrator of " Circe " remains the same whether he is describing " reality " or " fantasy ", while " Cyclops " involves two distinct narrators.) My point is simply that it is neither very accurate nor very helpful to say that the " content of Bloom's and Stephen's hallucinations and nightmares is objectified through the dramatic form " (13) ; in *Ulysses* the closest we ever get to a totally objective presentation of consciousness (or anything else) is the " Penelope " chapter, and even there the division of Molly's monologue into eight sections is the kind of artful effect that tends to control our response to the words we read.

If " Circe " is narration masquerading as drama it is important to recognize it as such and to be alert not only for the irony that inheres in this tension between the narrational and dramatic modes but also for the ironic effects that we expect in any story told by a clever, mischievous, and occasionally unreliable narrator. But who is this narrator ? I think it is most useful to regard the narrator as the artist in disguise. Pretending to be refined out of existence and to pare his fingernails, the artist is actually heavily involved in shaping and manipulating our view of the action in " Circe ". This, I take it is part of what Hayman means when he says " In 'Circe', the marginal playwright speaks to us from our own point of view, and the creatures whom we are fooled into seeing as grotesques discomfort us as part of an unnatural landscape into which we are drawn by a web of illusion " (14). The

---

(11) Hayman, p. 78.
(12) Weldon Thornton, *Allusions in Ulysses* (Chapel Hill : University of North Carolina Press, 1968), p. 359.
(13) Stanzel, p. 135.
(14) Hayman, p. 77.

technique is carried out further in *Finnegans Wake,* where the whole narration is more a commentary on a universal dream vision than an objective presentation of the dream itself. In this way the narrator or stage manager or arranger of " Circe " is a sort of first-draft version of the real dreamer of *Finnegans Wake :* the artist himself.

Patrick A. McCARTHY
University of Miami

The Paris Background
of FINNEGANS WAKE *

The Chairman began by drawing the meeting's attention to the sheets of notes which had been handed out. The first list of notes, which is given below, was a series of twenty possible references to the bridges of Paris all taken from the first chapter of Finnegan Wake.

Les Ponts de Paris, J.S. Atherton.

7.06,12	Taubling, Dobbelin	(P. Double + Dublin)
8.01	national	(P. National)
8.06	Redismemers invalids	(P. des Invalides)
8.25	the petty	(Petit P.)
9.25	solphereens	(P. de Solferino)
9.28	ousterlists	(P. d'Austerlitz)
9.35	royal	(P. Royal)
9.36	pettiest	(Petit P.)
10.04	hiena	(P. d'Iena)
11.23	allmichael	(P. St.Michel)
11.35	solly	(P. Sully)
12.06	marriedann	(P. Marie)
13.02	Royally	(P. Royal)
13.04	Dyoublong	(P. Double + Dublin in a French accent)
13.09	mitchel	(P. St.Michel)
13.14	the old butte new	(P. Neuf + Butt Bridge, Dublin, etc.)
13.27	desarted	(P. des Arts)
14.18	billy	(P. de Billy)
16.33	Louee, louee !	(P. St.Louis + P. Louis Philippe)
17.08	Load Allmarshy	(P. d'Alma)

Explaining these, the chairman said that one of Joyce's ways of inserting a subject into Finnegans Wake was to arrange items in a symmetrical pattern about a centre. Here, perhaps, the centre was on page 13 where someone says : " So This Is Dyoublong ? " This − I think − contains both Dublin in a French accent and the Pont Double. Ten lines down the page is " the old butte new " which

---

* Chairman : James S. Atherton, Lancashire, England ; Adaline Glasheen, Farmington, Conn., U.S.A. ; Maria Jolas, Paris ; Nathan Halper, Paris ; Stephen Heath, Jesus College, Cambridge ; Jacques Aubert, U. Lyon II.

combines the Butt Bridge in Dublin with Pont Neuf which, in spite of its name, is the oldest bridge in Paris. As you see Pont St. Michel is just above it and the Pont des Arts just below. At the foot of the same page is " national " which in the context can be taken as including a naming of Pont National. If you look through the others for yourselves you will see that they continue fairly thickly for a few pages on each side and fade away into faint resemblances almost too distorted to recognise.

A short discussion followed in which Nathan Halper pointed out that the references came in a chapter which began " riverrun ", and since the book is identified with Dublin and Paris, it is not surprising that the two are conflated ; the same thing happens in " eyeful howth entowerly " where the Eiffel Tower and Howth are conflated.

Adaline Glasheen then read some passages from Arthur Power's book *Conversations with James Joyce,* which had recently been published. One of the extracts concerned " an old church near Les Halles " which Joyce said reminded him " more than anything else " of his own writings. The church he referred to must be St-Eustache, and yet although the name Eustache comes twice in Finnegans Wake it does not seem to refer to this church. Joyce, as is well known, took a delight in weaving names into his book. Madame Jolas and her husband are probably being named on page 130, line 3 : " between youlasses and yeladst glimpse of Even ". On one level this is describing Joyce sitting between the two, Monsieur and Madame Jolas, and talking till late in the evening.

Nathan Halper then spoke on the appearance in the " Haveth Childers Everywhere " section of the names of the arrondissements and quartiers of Paris. He pointed out a great number of these, only a selection being included in the notes handed out at the meeting.

Les Arrondissements in " *H*aveth *C*hilders *E*verywhere ". 536.10 aroundisements. 531.12-26 Montmartre (Toulouse-Lautrec, la Goulue, Can-can, etc.) 532.35 opera-tops (Opéra). 534.08 ernst terooly (Reuilly). 534.08 Larry (St. Laurent). 535.5...7 hostel of the... city's (Hotel de Ville). 536.04 buttes (?). 536.12 ruely (Reuilly). 540.26 bourse. 546.06 genteelician (Elysée). 546.32 louvers (Louvre). 548.27 luxories (Luxembourg). 549.07 pacis (Passy). 551.24 upservatory (Observatoire). 553.13 gobelins. 553.12 templogues (Temple).

He said that references to Paris in other parts of Finnegans Wake tended to be largely biographical, but in the HCE section, which is about cities, allusions could be found to almost every city in the world. Once you have established the existence of a topic of this kind, he said, it is permissible to find examples in plays on words and in spellings which would be untenable without the presence of all the other less distorted examples. In the discussion that followed he pointed out that " Transocean atalaclamoured him " (p. 100.01) is naming *transition*. Ruth van Phul suggested that it also included the title of *Transatlantic Review*. In the chairman's opinion the meeting agreed with this suggestion but Nathan Halper dissented.

The chairman then introduced Dr. Stephen Heath to explain his research into some Parisian telephone numbers that seem to be mentioned in Finnegans Wake. A list of these was provided.

> *Quelques numéros de téléphone.* 275.17 'Phone number 17.69. 308.01 Gobble Anne : tea's set, see's eneugh (Gobelins dix-sept, six-neuf). 501.10 Cigar shank and Wheat (Ségur cinquante-huit). 501.11 Gobble Ann's Carrot Cans (Gobelins quarante-quinze) (These were first pointed out by Niall Montgomery several years ago). ? 233.31 zingo, zango, segur (0 5050 Ségur).

Stephen Heath explained that he had searched in the Parisian telephone directories for the appropriate years for all the numbers on the list which J.S. Atherton had supplied. One or two of these proved untraceable.

308.01 Gobble Anne : tea's set, see's eneugh ; and 275.17 'Phone number 17.69 turned out to be GOBELINS 17.69 Aux Petits Fabricants, 30, Avenue d'Italie, Paris-13e. This is a shop specializing in " vêtements, imperméables, cuirs ", clothes, rainwear and leather goods.

501.10 Cigar shank and Wheat.

SEGUR 50.08, Imprimeries Studium, 22, rue des Volontaires Prolongée, Paris-15e. (*" Studium "* appears in a book-publishing context at 123.18).

The number can also be read in two other ways :

SEGUR 58.00, Etablissements Simon, 24, rue Violet, Paris-15e. This is a shop " teinturerie, dégraissage ", dyer and dry-cleaner.

SEGUR 00.58, was the number of an " avocat " named Valière, 33, rue du Champs de Mars, Paris-7e.

SEGUR 50.50 (" zingo, zango, segur ") proved difficult to trace and may not have been in use. The nearest traceable is SEGUR 50.00 which is the number of a dentist in rue Frémicourt, Paris-15e.

In Dr Heath's opinion none of the numbers of Joyce's friends appeared. The dentist's number might be relevant to the " zingo " passage. While on the subject of directories, there was a Madame Veuve Emile Puard living at the time in 7, rue St-Just, Paris-17e. She may be the person named at 184.31 " La Mère Puard ". Directories of the time also list under the name Joyce, as well as James and George, a Tessa Joyce, Art. Lyr. (i.e. artiste lyrique.) She could be referred to at 278 n3 : " When I'm Enastella and am taken for Essastessa... ".

A discussion followed in which several allusions to Paris from the list provided by Louis Mink * were mentioned. It was suggested that, since Joyce did not mention the name of St. Eustache's church to Arthur Power, he had forgotton its name himself, and since the church is often referred to by Parisians as " Notre Dame des Halles " it could be included in the name *" Notre Dame du Bon Marché "* (112.32). Doubts were raised as to the relevance of this to the context.

---

* Through the kindness of Professor Louis Mink the references to Paris in his *Gazetteer of " Finnegans Wake "*, which was to be published in 1978, were made available to the meeting.

The session ended with the chairman remarking that many of Joyce's descriptions of Dublin and the Liffey included allusions to Paris and the Seine. He thought that Joyce was saying this − among other things − when he wrote that one of Anna Livia's garments was " sequansewn " (208.17) for the word conflates sequins and Sequana, the Latin name for the Seine.

James S. ATHERTON

" *Joyce and Politics* "

The often repeated assumption that Joyce was indifferent to politics misrepresents him. It comes from the simplistic notion that politics means voting in elections, but such political gestures were meaningless so long as Ireland was under British subjection, and in any case Joyce lived outside the polling area. He shows himself to be political in the substance and texture of his work. Stephen Dedalus concludes *A Portrait* by promising 'to forge in the smithy of my soul the uncreated conscience of my race', and in so doing he defines the artist's role as a social and political one. Likewise Joyce, more radical than Homer or Shakespeare, declined to accept the world as he found it.

His early hope was in socialism, as he indicated in the first draft of *A Portrait of the Artist as a Young Man*. By socialism he meant a communal liberation of the spirit from domination by church and state. This liberation is in fact the burden of *Ulysses,* though the idea of socialism is no longer insisted upon. Joyce associated the church with false idealism, with sentimental love, with cruel moral oppression, with rule by terror. He associated the state (Ireland being then an occupied country) with brutal materialism, misuse of power, enslavement of the populace. These forces he found to be secretly in collusion, in that both regarded matter as vile. Part of his effort was to rescue matter − the physicality of bodies, the importance of proper living conditions − from disregard. He dissociated himself from those nationalists who simply wanted to perpetuate enslavement of body and soul under a patriotic banner.

Joyce was too wary of propaganda as an artistic danger to offer any program of political change. He allows Bloom to present one, rather blunderingly. But his own view − like that of Bloom and Stephen − envisaged Irish independence. This is implied in the stories of *Dubliners,* where the ignobility of Ireland under occupation by Britain and the Vatican is a principal theme which evokes its opposite. In *A Portrait,* it is closer to overt expression, because Stephen's sense of his mission includes a transformation of the ethos of Irish life. In *Ulysses* Joyce makes clear through the agencies of Bloom and Stephen his fierce opposition to church and state ; they steadily refuse to be intimidated by these forces. Joyce also allows Bloom to support eagerly the policies of Arthur Griffith, the one politician after Parnell whom Joyce could stand. The many references to Griffith throughout the book, culminating in the last chapter, must be taken as the novelist's bow to the politician. Joyce was completing his book just as the Irish Free State was being formed and Arthur Griffith elected its first president. Joyce saw the two events as connected : he was offering a new politics of mind and body, so that the emancipation of his compatriots through literature proceeded hand in hand with their emancipation by Griffith through politics. In his book's mirror they could find the conscience which they needed for a new and independent and secular state.

The subsequent tergiversations of Irish politics interested Joyce less, for his concern, like that of other people, began to shift to the international scene. Though he signed no petitions, Joyce made clear where his sympathies lay, by aiding perhaps a dozen Jews to escape from Nazi Germany and resettle in other countries. In *Finnegans Wake* he attempted to override immediate political differences by projecting a sort of universal politics. This was the interpenetration of nations and peoples by language. Once this was acknowledged, it would naturally follow that we are all members of the one body, socialists beyond the letter.

Richard ELLMAN
New College

Narrative in Ulysses

3rd and 4th levels

First day *

1. *Benstock.* — Today we are dealing with two very specific passages in the early portion of *Ulysses* (one from " Nestor " and one from " Calypso " which you have mimeographed copies of in front of you). Members of the audience will be observers and possibly participants in a conversation among people on this panel. We are encouraging your participation in this discussion providing your comments pertain specifically to the two passages we are examining this morning. We will begin by investigating the nature of narrative in the first passage, and I will ask James Naremore to begin and from then on panel participants can get in where they find space.

2. *Naremore.* — I'd like to try to make a distinction which might be useful as a place to begin, a formal distinction rather than a critical analysis of this passage. When a storyteller tells a story, whether orally or in written form — any kind of storyteller, whether we're talking about Homer or James Joyce or Irving Wallace or whoever —, he has a choice of using language in two ways. This is a very old distinction, a distinction that I think originates with the Greeks talking about Homer. The storyteller can use language to directly report a linguistic phenomenon — that is, he can use language to report to us what two characters say to one another or what a character might say to himself in the form of sentences inside his mind, or in the case of the second passage we're going to talk about this morning, the linguistic phenomenon reported is a letter from Milly to her father. In this case, the storyteller is bringing words, the fact of words, directly into the mouth of the character.

---

* Participants : Ulrich Schneider, Therese Seidel, James Naremore, David Hayman, Breon Mitchel, Roy Gottfried, John Hagopian, Jean Paris. Chairperson : Shari Benstock.

The storyteller can also use language in another way (I think the Greeks called it the mimetic way), and this second method is opposed to that first method. It is impossible to bring this table, for instance, directly into a fictional world, but we can use language to imitate the table in some way. The medium of language is used to convey through imitation some non-linguistic phenomena — and this distinction is important. This method enables us to talk about various kinds of sentences in the passage at hand. For example, it is easy to see sentences of the first type where we're reporting about linguistic happenings. In the first passage on pp. 28-29 there is a brief conversation between Stephen and a student in the classroom : " Do you understand me now ? Yes, sir" . These are clearly sentences of the first type — linguistic phenomena. The same circumstance is true in the second passage, the brief conversation between Bloom and Molly, and also in the letter from Milly. These are sentences of the first type. There are also very clear examples in these passages of sentences of the second type, where language is being used to report not linguistic events but non-linguistic events. For example, there's a clear example on pp. 65-66 when Bloom begins to eat his morning meal : " then he put a forkful into his mouth, chewing with discernment the toothsome pliant meat ". Clearly this description is not of anything a character said aloud or thought to himself in his mind. It's not a report of a linguistic phenomenon. It is, however, an imitation because in order to say " chewing with discernment the toothsome pliant meat ", your mouth has to masticate exactly the way Bloom is slowly chewing the meat. This is clearly a sentence of the second kind : a mimetic sentence.

There is a third category of sentences which might also be useful to keep in mind because it causes lots of argument about narrative when narrative is being described closely. This third category includes those sentences where the function of language is ambiguous, where we're not certain whether the thing recorded in the sentence is a linguistic phenomenon or a non-linguistic phenomenon. Many examples of this kind of ambiguous sentence are present here ; in fact, the very first sentence in the first passage is one of these kinds of sentences : " Across the page the symbols moved in grave morrice, in the mummery of their letters, wearing quaint caps of squares and cubes ". It is uncertain whether this is the recording of a verbal event or whether this is some kind of semi-verbal event ; some of these words may occur in Stephen's mind or the narrator may be telling us this indirectly. The narrator may be using narrative in some mimetic way. And many of the quarrels in descriptive analysis of narration involve this kind of ambiguous sentence. The sentence, whether or not we agree that it is a direct thought by Stephen Dedalus, tells us a lot about Stephen, and it is clearly a perception that Stephen has in his mind. Stephen is a very literary young man, and it is appropriate to have a literary sentence here with unusual word order, not the word order one would use in excited emotional speech, and least of all in the excited emotional of one's mind. There is a rather elaborate syntax in this sentence. Stephen may, in fact, be saying that sentence to himself. Since he's a writer, perhaps he composes little sentences like this in his mind. In any case, it is appropriate to him. It tells us something about his diffidence, his coolness, his rather prissy way of thinking about things. It is also, because he is an esthete, appropriate to his nostalgia for medieval Catholicism, that sort of *fin de siècle* air that runs all through this sentence: "grave morrice", "quaint caps", "mummery", that sort of thing. All of this is appropriate to Stephen Deladus' character. Like any good satanist, Stephen Deladus is nostalgic in many ways for the very Catholic hierarchy that he has rebelled against and he carries that paraphernalia around with him. It's very typical of the 19th century that he represents.

3. *Hayman.* — I like your introduction very much. The first sentence in the first passage is clearly in the style of the narrative. This is the voice of the narrator, as far as I can see. It is a narrative which is consistent in the first part of the book and one of the ways we can tell that this is the narrator is that the sentence plays with sound and meter so much. You don't get this in Stephen's thought. Stephen's thinking is much less formed in this sense. Although I do agree this first sentence is obviously reflecting Stephen's thought, it is almost in a kind of *style indirect libre,* but it is not really that of stream of consciousness. What you actually have is a series of metrical lines which make this a very delightful passage to read. Also, rather than talking about Catholicism here, I think we could talk about the implications of mathematics — the fact that these are Arabic numerals. What Stephen is doing — as usual — is symbolising, and what he is taking over from and picking up on the Arabic origin of numbers, going into the morrice dance (which, of course, is a dance of Arabic origin, but which is an English dance also), a mummery dance, a dance that is related to festivals, farcical events — usually around Christmas time, but other times, too. It is a " grave morrice ", it is a kind of mockery of its actual quality, which isn't necessarily " grave ". And it is interesting that the figures are wearing " quaint caps of squares and cubes " ; these are almost characters out of a painting by Klee. First of all, there are certainly no caps ; there are perhaps squares, but certainly no cubes. You get a falsified perspective here.

Audience; — But there are squares and cubes here — these are algebraic equations that Stephen is looking at and he sees the numbers in their mathematical context as squares and cubes. In mathematics you square and cube numbers. This is directly related to the algebraic problem here.

4. *Hayman.* — Yes, but we see caps and squares and cubes. You're quite right, we have the squares and cubes in the numbers, but we also have the hats and we project from there to the other kinds of squares and cubes.

5. *Hagopian.* — I don't like to disagree, but I do. It seems important to me to understand this passage as not merely the narrator's rendition of Stephen's thoughts, but Stephen's own articulation of it — that is to say, this is pure stream of consciousness. I think the clue to this is in the opening passage that follows the one marked for us : " Like him was I, these sloping shoulders, this gracelessness ".

The first person pronoun here indicates that this is Stephen's mind at work. This is important because what Stephen is doing is translating the effect of history into poetry. And that he can do this is already evident. Another clue is his concern with the Moors and the Arabic numbers and how they are manifested in the " here and now " of his relationship with his student, Sargent. But the *" Amor matris "* which occurs after the dialogue is also prompted by Stephen's preoccupation with his mother and his problem with his mother, and this too would be characteristic language for him to use in thinking about it − Latinate church language for that sort of thing. I don't have any difficulty seeing this passage as Stephen's, but I have a problem elsewhere − that is, I tried to work out whether or not there was any consistency in the shifts from the first person pronoun to the third person pronoun, and it seemed to me that the cue was that whenever we were having Stephen's thoughts registered, we have the first person pronoun ; whenever we have his actions and gestures registered, there is the third person pronoun. " He moved ", " he watched ", " he said " − indicating Stephen's behavior. There is one line at the top of p. 25 that still troubles me, however : " with envy he watched their faces " (the students' faces). Is Stephen aware of his envy ? If he is, then the stream of consciousness is maintained successfully ; but if he isn't, then the mind of the narrator is registered and we do have an outside consciousness observing what Stephen and the students are doing and that breaks the consistency of the stream of consciousness in this passage.

6. *Hayman.* − Why do you insist on the stream of consciousness ?

7. *Hagopian.* − I don't insist on it, I'm trying to figure it out.

8. *Hayman.* − Well, let's figure it out again. " Across the page the symbols moved in grave morrice ". Now you're saying that Stephen's thinking this line − is that right ?

9. *Hagopian.* − I think that is what is happening, yes − that Stephen is perfectly capable, in a detached way, of observing himself and the situation in which he is and translating it into poetry.

10. *Hayman.* − In the past tense ?

11. *Mitchell.* − If I could come in here. There is a distinction made in narrative technique which is generally pretty clear − between third-person narration, straightforward and simple as we are used to it in novels, and interior monologue which is usually grammatically signaled by the first person and by the present tense. But what we have here is something in between ; it's the thought of Stephen presented in the past tense but still in his language, with his feeling for language. The Germans have a word for this sort of narrative which they call *erlebte Rede*. It is recognizable precisely by being third person, past tense, yet in the language and thought of the person whose thoughts are being described. In

English it has been suggested by Dorrit Cohn that we might call it narrated monologue, to give this sense that there is a narrator who is narrating the inner thoughts of the person. To me it seems to solve the dilemma somewhat to see this passage as that rather straightforward use of narrated monologue.

Audience. — I'm not very happy about Prof. Naremore's use of " linguistic " in his introduction. I think that it's a bit misleading and is a rather loose use of " linguistic ". It would be more profitable, perhaps, to restructure your dichotomy in terms of a universal narrative — but there's no time for that. We're trying here to pinpoint something which cannot be. Labelizing this as indirect narrated monologue (as I think it can be labeled) admits that it is a deliberate sentence. You never know what the center is and this is deliberate on the part of the author. It creates an hallucinatory effect from the narrative point of view.

12. *Paris.* — I was just going to say something that you have said better. I agree with you that it's quite difficult to establish any precise, pure level of narration here because in a way that distinction between meta-linguistic statements and mimetic statements, etc., is precisely what Joyce is against. Rather consider this as indirect narrative or inner level monologue, we should indeed see that language here is speaking for itself, and I would now like to slightly displace the focus of the discussion. This passage is one of the first appearances in *Ulysses* of a kind of reference to the book itself, and perhaps instead of isolating that passage, we should begin by putting it in its context. Now this is the first time, or one of the first times, that Joyce is referring to the whole construction of his own novel. It is easy to see that the symbols which move in " grave morrice " across the page also move in the mind of the reader, up to a point. We have not found up to this point very much help from the author, but here comes that sentence : " Waiting always for a word of help ". It seems to me that this reference to the grave morrice, the symbolic mathematics, is in fact a reflection of the novel upon itself — that Joyce is telling us in a way that the whole model of the book is established there : " Give hands, traverse, bow to partner ". This is going to happen to Stephen and Bloom all day long — they are going to traverse, bow to each other, and withdraw.

Beginning right from this passage we have something, a kind of indication about his own style, something I would call introvert-extrovert. Here is mummery (this is perhaps " memory " ; due to the fact that I'm French — in the word " mummery " I hear " get thee to a nunnery ", the allusion to *Hamlet* and to memory also — all blended into just one word, just like the end of the passage " swaddling bands " refers to Blake's wellkown title " Infant Sorrow "). So it's almost impossible to isolate that passage without immediately seeing it expanding in all directions, which is the very mosaic of the whole novel.

13. *Mitchel.* — I'd like to reply to one thing that might be helpful here. If you're talking about the way in which this passage is written, rather than what

this passage means or how it can be interpreted, then it is interesting to me that the narrative techniques employed, whatever you want to call them, employ a purposeful ambiguity. Whenever an author wants to be ambiguous there is confusion between the narrator and narrated monologue. There is nothing unusual about this. This is a standard sort of narrative technique. What makes this unusual, in fact, is the langage and what the language means, but not the narrative technique itself. And I'd like to add here that when you speak of Joyce trying to break down distinctions of this sort I think that is what makes Joyce's unusual from the point of view of narrative technique : it is the clarity with which he separated the distinction between third person and inner monologue so often in the novel, combining third person and interior monologue in the same paragraph very clearly.

14. *Benstock*. – We began a few minutes ago with John Hagopian saying that he felt in this passage we were getting the straight stream of consciousness from Stephen throughout, and now we're arguing the opposite of that extreme. Perhaps there is a question as to the extent to which we are getting the kind of thing we've called " stream of consciousness " for so many years. Now we seem to have become involved with the ambiguities of the third person narrator.

If we look at just this first paragraph, is there any point at which, panel members, we seem to be totally, completely, unambiguously, inside what would be called Stephen's stream of consciousness ? Or are we always going back and forth between something we might call third person narrator – which seems sometimes to step closer to Stephen and other times to step back from him. What do you think ?

15. *Paris*. – Well, it's a question of distance. This language established itself at a certain distance of (or from) itself : whether we are close to the subject or close to the object. And the point here is something I forgot to say earlier : this passage is introduced precisely by the ignorance of the reader, so to speak. Sargent here stands for the reader of *Ulysses* and he has to be helped, to be briefed, about the technique of the narrative. In other words, this passage should be an answer to the questions that are piling up in the mind of the reader : what is this book about ? I don't understand anything – no more than Sargent understands algebra. So there is a negative statement : the reader must be helped. And there is a positive statement answering that sort of void – as if the whole passage was called for by the ignorance and the inability of the reader to solve the problem facing him with this novel.

16. *Seidel*. – You just suggested, Shari, that we should look for one passage where we can say clearly whether it is Stephen's interior monologue or not. I think it is not in this passage, but in the one that follows : " Like him was I, these sloping shoulders ", and so on. I think the only signal that we can find indicating interior monologue is the stylistic reference to the first person. We know explicitly whose point of view we share ; whereas in the passage we have been looking at

previously, we don't. The author seems to avoid reference to the first person, to mood, even to number. Most of the time he uses non-finite verbal forms which give this ambiguous appearance to the sentence. He does not say " I was doing ", or " I am doing ". We are given just the participles instead (wearing, mocking, shining, flashing, gone too from the world). Indication of tense (as could be given through a form of the auxiliary like " was "or " is ") is avoided. " Give hands, traverse, bow to partner " can be both : description of the symbols' movements as they appear in Stephen's mind (" they " is left out) and also imaginary dancing instructions (either seen through Stephen's or the narrator's point of view), in which case the verbal form is in the imperative.

17. *Hayman.* – There is a shift in distance there, I think. You are moving closer to Stephen as the paragraph progresses. You may even be moving closer to the shape of his thought when you get to something like " gone too from the world ". You have a kind of immediacy which you don't have in the earlier passages. And I think that you can point to this as a kind of development – and it is ambiguous – deliberately so.

18. *Seidel.* – Yes, Joyce avoids finite verbal forms which could show the exact point of view.

19. *Hayman.* – I'd like to reiterate something I said earlier about the shape of the narrator himself – that is, we do have a kind of persona here and we can confuse the persona with Stephen or with Joyce, if we wish, but certainly at this time and in these types of passages, where they relate to Stephen especially, we have a great deal of language play, of verbal play, a great deal of metrical play and alliteration. These are all markers for us too of the kind of figure we have here and it is an important figure to note because he disappears later on.

20. *Benstock.* – Are you saying the kind of figure that is Stephen or the kind of figure that is the narrator ?

21. *Hayman.* – The narrating persona.

22. *Benstock.* – And he disappears later on. How far later on do you think ?

23. *Hayman.* – At " Cyclops ". You don't have him after " Cyclops " except for a few passages.

24. *Naremore.* – One of the things that interests me – and we have to go to the second passage, the Bloom passage, to illustrate this. Bloom is less obviously a self-conscious character and we have more sentences in the Bloom passage which seem to be a greater distance away from the consciousness of the character, which seem to be a rather traditional point at which the narrator stands outside and describes the character. One of the most obvious passages is when Bloom goes

down the stairs and we talk about his " flurried stork's legs " stepping hastily down the stairs. It appears to be a description applied from outside, by the narrator. But one of the sentences interests me, something about style, and I offer this point humbly, because I'm not confident about it. In the penultimate paragraph, just before Milly's letter where Bloom sits down to eat, there are sentences like " prodding a prong of the fork under the kidney he detached it and turned it turtle on its back ". This is not inner monologue, it is a report of what is happening at this moment and it has those very characteristics we noticed in the Stephen passage, of being metrical, of having alliteration, " prodding a prong of the fork, turned it turtle on its back ". You get the sense always, if not of a narrative personality, the way you think of a narrative personality with Lawrence or Virginia Woolf, at least of somebody manipulating language with great skill, great mimetic skill, and it implies a personality behind this narrator. There is always in fact a discrepancy between the very beauty with which the *mot juste* is found and the mundane ordinary things that are being talked about. I don't know whether language could be said to be used as a defense here against the ordinary trivial subject matter, or whether language could be said to try to redeem the everyday in a rather romantic way, almost. But in any case you do feel the personality of someone here present, and I think this happens frequently in the early portions of the book.

25. *Hagopian*. – I want to disagree most emphatically with that. I picked out the same passage you did and came to exactly the opposite conclusions about it. The first person pronoun indicates the consciousness of Bloom at work here (" Three and six I gave for the frame. She said it would look nice over the bed "). But when I got to that passage about stepping hastily down the stairs with the flurried stork's legs I said that it broke the stream of consciousness because Bloom is surely not aware of his legs that way. But further on p. 66 you see that he is well aware of Milly's slim legs running up the stairway. Then I remembered that Bloom, author of the book, is conscious of women's legs and legs in general. Then it struck me that it is not at all unlikely that as Bloom hurries up the stairs he thinks of his own legs as awkward stork's legs – that is consistent.

26. *Naremore*. – Let me agree with that ambiguity. I should have admitted it was there.

27. *Hagopian*. – Secondly, about the turtle. Again I thought about flipping the kidney and it looks like a turtle and I thought in whose mind, in whose consciousness does that kidney look like a turtle ? Is it the narrator's or is it Bloom's ? And then I recalled that all through the book, Bloom is consistently aware of animals and their appearance and movements. He's an animal-oriented man.

28. *Paris*. – That doesn't matter at all.

29. *Hagopian.* – It matters to me.

30. *Paris.* – It doesn't matter who is talking because language is speaking, as Lacan pointed out yesterday.

Audience. – But the question is : is there a narrator ? And when there is a narrator, whether you identify the narrator or not, you have to be concerned with what the narrator is reporting. When the narrator is on a theme, you have a theme reported, and where the language is supposed to be recording action, action is reported. And what Prof. Naremore has been saying before is that you have a narrator engaged in a mimetic act, trying to make language imitate action, and what you, Prof. Paris, are doing is suggesting that this is all verbal. I'm very sympathetic. I think this is a difficulty. The world of Joyce is made up of words that imitate actions and this is what we have here and in the opening sentence (" Across the page... " : we have a narrative imitation of the visual picture that occurs in Stephen's mind. And so in answer to what you were saying before, Shari, when you asked when are we in Stephen's mind, my answer would be that we are in Stephen's mind here (in this first passage), but he's not verbalising, he's picturing, vizualizing it.

Audience. – We suggest that the opening line of Homer's *Odyssey* provides the clue to the narrative structure of *Ulysses*. There are three figures mentioned : there's the man, there's me, and there's you.

31. *Paris.* – What I'd like to suggest is that the narrator is a character in this story, who happens to disappear in the way many other characters do. But essentially what one finds, and I'm in agreement with this idea of the transcendent muse mentioned earlier, is that there is a manipulator of some kind, and I don't mean a manipulator of scene in a paragraph, but a manipulator of language. The phrase has come from someone on this panel. I'd like to suggest that this manipulation of language is the very first thing we observe – independent of the meanings.

Audience. – " Tell me news of the man ". I think we move away from the general issues – news, sources of information – we move to a far greater distance than is actually necessary. Hence for example in " Ithaca ", the news is described in the same flat tone irrespective of the question – " What happened when Bloom turned... ? " I'm very much in agreement that language is indeed not the only medium operating here, but is actually the *substance and fabric* of *Ulysses*.

32. *Roy Gottfried.* – Of the words in this first section, for example, " Across the page the symbols moved... " we immediately sense language which is being turned out of the order normally expected : the symbols move across the page. We sense that there is a manipulation which is taking the actual words themselves and twisting them out of shape, pulling them apart, putting them in different order. I'd

like to suggest that this arrangement of normal syntactic order in a way provides just the openings and opportunities that combine narrator and character. It's one of the reasons why we have so much trouble distinguishing them : at the level of syntax these are constantly being bounced, being paralleled. Look for example at the sentence " Waiting always for a word of help his hand moved faithfully the unsteady symbols... " Right away we're completely disordered. " Moved the unsteady symbols faithfully " is probably what we would expect. We would like to say this is the narrator, but it is language manipulated simply. Can we really say that this is Stephen : " with her weak blood and wheysour milk ? " I would like to suggest that these sorts of distinctions between character and narrator on the level of narration and interior monologue, are in a way brought together, or brought about, by a syntax in *Ulysses* which is constantly manipulated and in which we can see some kind of enormous control over all that happens.

Audience. − I think linguistics have more to say in this discussion than has so far been said. Namely, I'm surprised that there has been no mention made of overt meaning and covert meaning. What is very clear to me is that there is some kind of assertion versus free supposition. There are some kinds of circuit centers versus pre-supposed centers of the statement. The pre-supposed center of a particular sentence is what troubles us in looking at this passage.

33. *Schneider.* − I always thought Mr. McIntosh in " Hades " was the most mysterious character in *Ulysses,* but actually the most mysterious seems to be the narrator. This morning Father Boyle gave us the metaphor of the ventriloquist and now the term " manipulator " has been brought in. Such terms strike me, however, as just variations of the word " narrator " ; they don't provide any illumination about how this being actually functions.

34. *Hayman.* − Well, where do you see him in the second half of the novel ?

35. *Schneider.* − We don't see him. We don't see him much in the first part as a character, which is a very important thing. But you never lose the feeling that there are two consciousnesses at the same time, and out of their interaction results a great deal of the irony, ambiguity or whatever you may call it. But there is always *someone* who arranges everything, who is beyond the perspective of any character and no matter what you call it you are bound to acknowledge that it exists.

36. *Hayman.* − I didn't say the arranger disappears in the second half. Actually there he becomes much more obvious. What actually happens in the second half is this voice that I've pointed to here, which disappears except in a few passages. In other words, you don't have the so-called, the apparent, objective narrative − it's not objective at all, but apparently objective. Someone we trust, someone who speaks with a certain accent with which we are familiar.

37. *Schneider*. – But regardless of whether he stays or goes, what can we say about this character ? What sort of fellow is he ? Is it James Joyce there ? Tell us something about it.

38. *Hayman*. – It's not James Joyce, I hope. Let's say that you have a character, or a figure, or a persona, or a voice, which tends to take different distances to different characters. For example, Bloom – the voice is much more distant from Bloom than from Stephen. It's quite a shock when we move from the narrative discourses to Bloom's discourses ; whereas it's actually rather gentle, the movement from the narrator's discourse to Stephen's discourse. So there is a shift there, but it's remarkable that it stays so similar throughout, even though it does change throughout from chapter to chapter. The tonality of the chapter still dictates the tonality of the narrator.

Audience. – When someone is speaking, Americans call him a narrator. Prof. Paris, you are an excellent mediator between Americans and the French point of view. The French say language speaks for itself – sometimes that irritates me. I'd like you to mediate a little more between us. Would you say language speaks for itself to the extent that you can eliminate the hypothesis of the narrator ?

39. *Paris*. – No, but I think decoding *Ulysses* in terms of characters, in terms of subjects, here so-and-so is speaking, here is Joyce, here is someone else, is missing the whole point. It seems to me that Joyce has given up the theory of subject so to speak, and the best man to answer your question would not be me, but Lacan. What he said yesterday.

Audience. – I understand you better than Lacan, so I would like to know the point that the Americans have missed.

40. *Paris*. – Well, certainly I'm not going to give a lecture on Lacan, but the point he tried to make yesterday was that unconsciousness is structured like a language. This is Lacan's hypothesis. In other words, language is the unconscious, so to speak. The organization of language is the unconscious. The very fact that we learn a language at a time when we have no control over our consciousness at all, you see, that is the starting point. Now if we admit that premise we have to understand that the subject, the one who says " I ", is certainly not the same as the " I " that you hear. In other words, that's putting it in barbaric terms. The subject of the enunciation is not the subject of the enunciated no more than " I " is " me ". I have a very nasty question I would like to ask. We know, for instance, that language operates at several levels in *Ulysses*. But there is one level that has been missed up to this point : It is, what is Bloom doing at the very same time as Stephen is helping Sargent ? Does anybody know what Bloom is doing at the same time as Stephen is helping his little pupil with the algebra problem ? Because that might have an incidence on what he thinks here. They think at the same time of

the same things. They are linked by this very strong telepathy which takes place only in the mind of Joyce.

41. *Hayman.* – It's not always the same time.

42. *Paris.* – Not always. But I would like to ask the people who know *Ulysses* better than I : What is Bloom doing at that very moment ? Is he cooking his breakfast ? I think not. He's beyond that point. He's on his way to the funeral ? That might have an incidence on this scene, if we look carefully at the text. At that very precise minute, Bloom might be thinking of money, or avarice, or the Middle East or something, which determines Stephen thinking that way at that precise moment.

43. *Hayman.* – I don't think these parallels like you're describing them exist.

44. *Paris.* – These two men, Bloom and Stephen, are two faces of the same character, so to speak.

45. *Hayman* – They are, but I don't think these parallels exist in the way you're describing them.

46. *Paris.* – The son is co – existent with the father. Stephen says that all along the walk on the beach in the library scene.

47. *Hayman* – Jean Paris has mentioned an interesting parallel. I think it is worth noting here that we have two teaching situations and that is certainly one parallel between Stephen and Bloom, and you'll notice that they teach in very different ways – which is a symptom of the kind of relationship they have. It's an antagonistic symbiosis, if you wish. And it's amusing to see how Bloom works out the method by which he'll teach Molly, whereas Stephen doesn't even worry about the method by which he'll teach the boys. It's almost as though Bloom is filling in a lacuna in Stephen's thought process.

48. *Mitchell.* – But strangely enough the narrator mimics each character he describes. So the narrator and character have come close to the point of being synonymous and it happens as well in Bloom's own thought : " an example would be better. An example ", he thinks. When he actually speaks to Molly which is a recognizable fact, he says, " They used to believe you could be changed into an animal or a tree, for instance. What they called nymphs, for example ". The teaching situations have been brought into juxtaposition with each other even though they're really disparate in regard to Stephen and Bloom themselves.

49. *Schneider.* – The function of the narrator is never merely mimetic. I don't object to the word " mimetic " but it is not enough. So far, it seems to me,

we have been talking about the consciousness of the narrator and of the characters, but I think Jean Paris pointed out something important, namely a third dimension, the reader. It is the reader who draws conclusions about the first two and must provide a synthesis. Someone made an association between " mummery "-" nunnery "-" memory " for example ; that is the reader's activity which we have neglected so far.

50. *Paris.* – Right, and that's why I think we should not even use the word mimetic. It's down with Aristotle, I would say.

51. *Naremore.* – I don't want to get into a big discussion on Lacan, because I don't understand Lacan well enough, but the notion of the language speaking itself seems to be designed to give us help about the story without the intervention of some obvious personality, some spokesman coming into the story to hand us help. So that on the surface the language of the novel does appear to be speaking itself. I wonder if maybe that strategy isn't determined by Joyce's desire to hide himself, to deny that my language betrays something about me, about my unconscious, about the determinants of my life, and so the whole narrative technique here is an elaborate desire on Joyce's part to conceal himself from us as readers, to make us believe that this novel is walking along by itself and by our intervention and our interpretation. And our task is to reassert *that* Joyce to show how his language speaks himself.

52. *Paris.* – If you will allow me to add just one more sentence from Lacan, I would say that the function of language is not to reveal, it's to conceal.

53. *Naremore.* – I agree, and this is language which is designed to conceal far more than ordinary language does and our task is to find out what.

54. *Paris.* – Yes, but in doing so you are applying to Joyce the same kind of method that you would apply to Dickens or to Proust, and this is not consistent – this I don't think is consistent with the project of the whole matter.

55. *Gottfried.* – I just want to add something in response. This paradox is so observable in a narrative which at one and the same time breaks up its own language to obscure the difference between the character and narrator and yet absolutely asserts itself by breaking up language – the paradox exists on the lexical level as well as on the idealogical level of the Eucharist or the artist's own process.

56. *Hayman.* – I'm just a little worried about this conversation between the reader and the writer that's going on. I don't think it exists.

57. *Paris.* – Can I just read the passage which is the most Lacanian of the whole paragraph this morning : " Flashing in their mocking mirrors the obscure

soul of the world, a darkness shining in brightness which brightness could not comprehend ". It's right there.

Audience. – Maybe I don't agree. The author – or arranger of this book – reveals himself through the language. Just as Stephen says he reads the signatures of all things – that's the proof : " shut your eyes and see ".

Naremore's use of the word " mimetic " is used for objective reality. What you said earlier that Joyce would like to be known as the creator and not as Joyce the man with a biography is questionable. I'm not sure he would, but he is after all a human being – and books are written by people who live. What I was saying is that I understand the need for the kind of distinctions you've made about implied authors and things of that sort, but there is also a need to understand something about this man – his psychology, his culture, his political milieu – outside the idealízed, purely formal structure. I think it's important to have an awareness of the presence of an author – it's important also to try at least to postulate a James Joyce – somewhere.

Second day *.

58. *Benstock.* – We will begin today with the first page of " Circe ". We'll want to begin discussing connectives – if there are any – between the kinds of techniques that panel members and members of the audience isolated yesterday and what begins to happen as we move into the nightworld of Dublin, as opposed to the dayworld. Yesterday, in " Calypso " and " Nestor ", we isolated three different levels of narration : one involving characters speaking, one comprising a narrator narrating the events of the story, and another including what I think David Hayman called an " arranger " – i.e., something separate from the narrator's voice or the voices of the characters' speaking, a controlling or directional " voice " in the work. How do we begin to define the voices of " Circe " ?

59. *Hayman.* – There is a voice in " Circe ", a very careful voice – as distinct and precise as the voice we saw in the passage from " Nestor " yesterday. But this isn't precisely the same voice we had yesterday because it doesn't play with language in quite the same way. It isn't as full of alliteration ; there are not as many metrical tricks being played. In fact, there are very few – this is almost deliberately prosaic. However, it is so carefully controlled that we have a strong

---

* Participants : Ulrich Schneider, Thérèse Seidel, James Naremore, David Hayman, Breon Mitchell, John Hagopian, Liisa Dahl. Chairperson : Shari Benstock.

sense of someone very much in control. There is a kind of *persona,* but we're not immediately certain of what kind of *persona.* I don't think we ever know for certain what kind of *persona* operates in the second half of the book. Let's just look briefly at the opening of this passage :

The Mabbot street entrance of nighttown, before which stretches an uncobbled tramsiding set with skeleton tracks, red and green will-o'-the-wisps and danger signals. Rows of flimsy houses with gaping doors. Rare lamps with faint rainbow fans (U 429).

That's very nice. It illustrates the kind of command we expect of the voices that inhabit *Ulysses.* But there is something else going on, something which also occurred in the earlier passages yesterday : we notice in all these passages that there is a kind of slippage from level to level. And in Stephen's mind, for example, there is a sense of allusive elements − in the way he handles his own perceptions or the way in which his perceptions are projected by the narrative voice. First we have the numbers on the page (U 28) and then we move from the numbers as Stephen sees them on the page to what the numbers might signify in other dimensions − in terms of the history of man or the history of Europe or of the Arabs or in terms of dance. There are a whole variety of allusive elements presented. In other words, there exists even in the earliest chapters a kind of hallucinatory element − it is very slight and we accept it as naturalistic. Here, in " Circe ", we are sucked *into* it. Indeed, we don't know quite when the hallucinations begin − we can mark them, of course − but we really don't know quite when reality becomes hallucination or when hallucination becomes reality ; sometimes, for instance, Bloom's hallucination is something that really should be in Stephen's mind.

Throughout this chapter, we don't know quite when things occur and from the very start a naturalistic scene − and it is a naturalistic scene − is presented to us as though it were surrealistic (I use the word " surrealistic " loosely here because I don't really mean surrealistic in the restricted context). Consequently, it is not surprising that there have been critics of Joyce who have told us that what we really see in this first passage is just stunted men and women − literally − even though Joyce tells us that these are children, even though the text tells us these are children. I'm thinking of the production of " *Ulysses* in Nighttown " − in that version we actually get stunted creatures. In short, we are brought into the context that one frequently associates with expressionist plays, or with *Faust,* which was one of Joyce's models.

60. *Benstock.* − To summarize : what you're saying about this opening paragraph is that we approach the difficulties here by attempting to sort out a " reality " that is familiar to us from the kind of hallucinatory stream that the chapter presents.

61. *Hayman.* − No. The *joy* is in sharing in the hallucination rather than emphasizing its difficulty. I think we really get pulled into this hallucination, even

though it's true that we do also try to sort it out. But we have this double joy – the pleasure of the hallucination and the pleasure of seeing through the hallucination ; this is obviously a double exposure. We cannot be one place or the other altogether, so we enjoy this kind of flux of experience which is the flux of experience of " Circe ".

62. *Benstock.* – What happens, then, when you begin to get the dialogue between characters ? Is this something different ?

63. *Schneider.* – We must remember that there are many connections between this and the earlier chapters not only concerning the repetition of *leitmotifs* but also the technique. For instance, we find the animation of things through metaphors practised constantly in the earlier chapters : the symbols " move ", the cream is " sluggish ", the jet of the teapot " angry ". Now this principle is exploited even further ; everything is animated ; everything, as we are told in an earlier chapter, speaks in its own way.

64. *Dahl.* – May I just make a brief remark about these stage directions ? I see a close connection of these backstage directions with O'Neill's *Strange Interlude.* He used a lot of nominal sentences that produced a similar atmosphere. And I think Joyce is also expressionistic – as O'Neill's *Strange Interlude* certainly was – in emphasizing the essential which is personified by these characters, drawing out the quintessential in them.

65. *Naremore.* – One or two small things. You remark here that the stage directions are deliberately prosaic, David. There are one or two sentences here that I find deliberately not prosaic. For instance, " The swancomb of the gondola, highreared, forges on through the murk, white and blue under a lighthouse. Whistles call and answer " (U 429). This, to my ear, sounds very much like the chamber music that we've been hearing from Joyce's earliest writings and it recalls a style that Joyce began with. When I come to " Circe " I am still locked in the old-fashioned need to imagine who is hallucinating all this. Who does this world belong to ? And is it possible that we can make any correlatives between the fanciful things described here and something actually, physically, happening in nighttown ? I find it very difficult to do that. Yesterday we talked about the way in which Bloom and Stephen are sometimes thinking the same things, each expressing it in terms that " fit " with his mode of expression. It is possible to sort out who is thinking what, even though there may be a conjunction of *what* is thought. It is very difficult to sort out these kinds of narrative levels in a chapter like " Circe ". In the later chapters there seems to be a deliberately exploded narration, resulting in the frustration of the reader's rational desire to make connections, to single out a style, a narrator, an objective " event " going on in the world.

66. *Hayman.* – In this chapter the reader is becoming very much engaged

in an important personal experience – he isn't just " reading " the novel, he's experiencing it. Because of the technique we don't really know – objectively – what people are thinking or saying. We only get versions of what is happening, a slanted view (or views).

67. *Seidel.* – May I just say a word about the " Nestor " episode as we try to relate the " Circe " technique to techniques we observed yesterday. " Nestor " has a much stronger naturalistic level, which means that as readers we understand what is happening much easier than we do when confronted with the technique of " Circe " where the naturalistic level is obscure to us. It is possible in " Nestor " to separate thoughts, from spoken words, from the narrative line, from action rendered through observation rather than through spoken language – the " reality " is more easily tangible in the earlier chapters.

David Hayman has described the difference between " Nestor " and " Circe " as a problem of distance : " Nestor " allows us to " think ", whereas " Circe " invites us to " hallucinate ". Although this describes a difference between the two chapters, the description also uses a common denominator : the intended effect upon the reader and the reader's response.

When we keep the category " effect upon the reader " for a moment, we can try to describe the relationship berween the earlier chapters (" Nestor " and " Calypso ") and the later ones (" Circe " and " Ithaca ") on the one hand, and a kind of technical and functional consistency the later chapters have, on the other hand. It has become clear, that we cannot describe " Circe " or " Ithaca " satisfactorily in merely mimetic terms (" What happens...? "), nor in terms of narrative stance (" From whose point of view is it told ?). We have to see that both chapters are also poetological ones : That is to say, they tell us something about how *Ulysses* is made and furthermore about how literature and conventional literary reality is made (and understood). And they may even tell us something about extra-literary reality and our conventional perception of it – this holds good mainly for " Circe ".

It is true, " Nestor " can also be read as a poetological chapter – as Jean Paris has pointed out : " traverse, bow to partner "... etc. can be understood as the description of *Ulysses* itself and its characters. But the difference is : we don't have to understand it like this. In the earlier chapters we can do without the poetological level – at least on first reading. But how could we understand " Circe " – unless we claim with John Hagopian that Joyce had gone mad by the time he wrote it – without the assumption of some consistency, preferably that of a poetological or ontological kind ?

68. *Hayman.* – We might modify slightly what you're saying : in the earlier chapters the reader is permitted to " think " (for himself) ; in " Circe " he is involved with the experience and is not permitted to step back too far from it, to become too objective in his rational analysis of it – at least, not on first readings.

69. *Seidel.* – Yes, I agree ; but I think I would emphasize the common traits of these two chapters rather than the differences. There are two levels, at least, in the " Nestor " episode and it is not always very easy to distinguish between the reality outside and the reality inside – that is to say in Stephen's mind.

In " Circe " Joyce uses the avowedly most objective literary form : that of drama. And he uses it to transport the most subjective contents : Stephen's and Bloom's thoughts, visions, hallucinations. And even that level is sometimes transcended, so that we cannot say whose consciousness is presently dramatized : Stephen knows things that realistically speaking he couldn't know, and so does Bloom. What we learn from this reading experience is that our conventional habit of distinguishing between subjective and objective, real-unreal, inner and outer world, fiction-non-fiction, etc., is not valid always. These distinctions are no longer valid – even if Joyce has made use of them himself in order to establish Stephen and Bloom as mimetic characters in our mind. The fact that we get confused now in " Circe " only shows that the literary convention of character-consistency has worked, that we expect the author to go on with it and we even become angry when he does not continue the illusion.

A similar thing happens in " Ithaca " – I would say, even more so. In " Circe ", we could always come up with an easy mimetic explanation (like : " It is the night world of " Circe ", everything can happen there "). But we cannot do so in " Ithaca ". Why does the chapter make use of a technique or literary form that is so adequate to Stephen (the question and answer game of the catholic catechism) to transport contents rather adequate to Bloom (pseudo-scientific reflections) ? Of course, both are mocked at by exaggerating these idiosyncracies of the two characters as they are by then well known to the reader.

70. *Hayman.* – The difference is the method. Here (in " Circe ") we are struck by the quality of the hallucination – and we experience it.

71. *Benstock.* – Could I ask the question from the opposite way around ? Who is it that is in control in " Circe " – who controls this " reality " or that " hallucination " ? Is this force something different than the narrator we isolated yesterday ?

72. *Hagopian.* – I think we're laboring to prove what seems to be obvious : no book writes itself. There is always an author who puts those words on the page, and he would like to think that his presence is sensed by any reader. There is truth in this assumption, of course, but it is not the primary *critical* concern. I am the kind of reader who is always asking who is ostensibly (not actually, because Joyce *actually* wrote these words) responsible for these words – i.e., who is presented as being responsible for these words ? And in the opening sections as well as in the final chapter, the Molly soliloquy, it seems quite clear that we have more or less pure stream of consciousness. In these sections the character is responsible for that language, this in turn leads the reader to question who is

feeling the experience presented, whose consciousness is being rendered by the language on the page. In this morning's panel on editorial problems in *Ulysses,* Michael Groden made an interesting observation that in his examination of the manuscripts he came to the conclusion that Joyce got tired of the stream of consciousness technique about 1919-1920 and began to fool around and intrude external consciousness and external controls of language which are not those of the characters but that of the narrator (Joyce, presumably) and that he did this while working on " Cyclops ". Then he had a major eye operation and had to stop work for a month and a half and after that his intrusions became wild. And what we have here is an example of this kind of intruding on the part of the narrator. The language and consciousness rendered is not that of any of the characters, it is that of the narrator. Pat McCarthy has pointed out that in " Circe " the hallucinations are not those of the characters but rather of the narrator. That statement has illumined this whole passage for me.

73. *Hayman.* – That darkens it for me, I'm sorry.

74. *Naremore.* – I think there is a sense in which the reader at this stage of the novel is being allowed to hallucinate about all the material in the novel, having successfully gotten himself to this point in *Ulysses.* So that when we get down to the middle of page 430 and hear Cissy Caffrey's voice it is startling. If you try to apply any logical rationale for Cissy Caffrey being at the Mabbot Street entrance to nighttown, you get nowhere. The chapter is full of this kind of bizarre information as though not only are we – at one level – dealing with this naturalistic phenomena far beyond obvious hallucination, but the book seems to be writing itself, letting itself hallucinate. And I think that Joyce consciously set about trying to deny the possibility of saying *who* is responsible for this hallucination. Sometimes it seems to be a character, sometimes it seems to be an unnamed narrator, sometimes it is just us participating with Joyce in the joy – or maybe the anxiety – of this underground world. We can take all the materials of the novel and go on a kind of trip with it in " Circe ".

75. *Hayman.* – Could I pick up on something that you were saying earlier, John ? I'm sorry to disagree so thoroughly with almost everything you say, but I disagree especially with what was said (as you quote it) in the other section – i.e., that Joyce said at some point that he was going to go wild and create a kind of narrative craziness. First of all, such an hypothesis doesn't work in terms of this novel. This is a whole, there is a continuance and continuing developing of style, there is a phasing in and out of effects – all highly controlled and deliberate – not accidental. So it is really absurd to think that Joyce suddenly, because he had an eye operation of all things, went wild with the narrative.

76. *Hagopian.* – Don't you experience, as I experience in reading this book, an enormous sense of relief from effort at perception when you reach Molly Bloom's soliloquy ? We're back in familiar territory ; it flows and we understand

and there are no problems anymore as there clearly are in the " Circe " episode, in the catechism episode, and so on. He's come back to the beginning, round again.

77. *Hayman.* – Sure, but what do you draw from that ? In a sense, this can be explained because we're leaving the night as morning approaches.

78. *Hagopian.* – OK, you're welcome to your justification for that. I have problems, say, with the catechism chapter. When I read it I ask myself : an experience is being rendered in a strange and unusual form – why this technique ? What is achieved by this technique ?

79. *Schneider.* – Your objections to the complications of technique in the later chapters have been answered in an article by Walton Litz called " The Genre of *Ulysses* ". What you are doing is to reduce the novel to some other level, and in doing so, you get only half of what Joyce intended. There is no point in saying that some chapters represent the " real " Joyce and the others represent the effects of an eye operation or the state of his deteriorated mind. *Ulysses* is of whole cloth and you have to accept it on its own terms. There are many ways in which Joyce prepared the reader in the earlier chapters for the difficulties in the ones to come.

It strikes me as important that Stephen constructs a piece of literary fiction and Bloom a scene from real life. To me the juxtaposition of the two scenes seems to comment not only on the characteristic differences between Stephen and Bloom but also, in an oblique way, on two different narrative modes which one might call loosely the symbolistic and naturalistic mode. Stephen's " construction " is a literary vignette which reminds me much of his – and Joyce's – epiphanies. We are told nothing about the identities of the characters which are referred to in the vaguest terms (" a young man " – " a young woman "). We never find out what goes on in the woman's mind or what is her relationship with the two men. The appropriate setting for this dim scene is twilight ; Bloom might find Stephen's epiphany " dreamy, cloudy, symbolistic " like the esthetes in " Lestrygonians ". In Bloom's " construction " of the scene of his father's death the data of time and place couldn't be more precise. It is told in the typical mode of " Ithaca " and we are spared no details. But we soon find out that in spite of all this effort to achieve scientific objectivity as many questions are left unanswered as in Stephen's sketch. There is, for example, no explanation for the puzzling question why Bloom's father bought a new hat on the day he committed suicide. It turns out that the detailed " naturalism " of Bloom's scene is a *trompe l'œil,* and this seems to me typical for the whole episode. In spite of all the overwhelming details, everything in the chapter remains seen as through a haze, and we never find out what " really " happens – just like in Stephen's symbolistic narrative. Thus the extremes meet – Stephen's epiphanies and Bloom's circumstantial precision. In both cases truth remains stranger than fiction, as we are told elsewhere in this chapter.

80. *Naremore.* – What strikes me as strange is the way " Circe " is almost a

commentary on the society in which we live. There is a kind of technique at work here which appears to be an attack on the bourgeois realist novel, the surface of that familiar 19th century novel. " Circe " and " Ithaca " shatter the normal positivist kind of novel in all sorts of ways. All of us, myself included, feel the need when we look at this warped surface to translate it back into some kind of realistic terms understandable to us. We feel compelled to do that. That is why such works as *The Skeleton Key* abound for *Finnegans Wake*. That's why we gather together to have panels like this one. I don't say that this is wrong, just that there is a real paradox in trying to take a surface that is counter to all realist traditions and translate it back into realist terms.

81. *Mitchell.* – What strikes me as unusual about the narrative technique in the " Circe " episode is simply its context – that is, that it occurs within a novel at all. A glance at Karl Kraus's *Die letzten Tage der Menschheit* (written in the final years of World War I) will reveal that an almost identical technique was employed. Whether a direct influence might be postulated is a separate question. The point here is that Kraus's work is called a drama (although he said it could only be produced in another world). If the " Circe " episode were not in a novel, we would simply see it as one further example of dramatic experimentation in the second decade of this century, with both expressionistic and surrealistic traits. The technique itself is not that unusual – that Joyce should employ the technique in a novel is. As in other instances, the significance of Joyce's action lies in the deliberate attempt to break through the rigid conventions of the 19th century novel, and to free the artist from his literary past.

82. *Hayman.* – The point seems to be a fairly simple one : what happens by the time we get to " Circe " is that we've been disconnected from our characters – even from their reality as well. Because what happens when we move into " Cyclops " and from there to " Wandering Rocks " is a major break with the novel in " realistic " terms. Suddenly we find ourselves (in " Cyclops ") in the mind of a character we've never seen before. There is an archetypal narrative voice telling us truths, modulated strangely, that throw us off balance. We try to sort out the truth from what seem to be lies or distortions. And besides all of this there are innumerable intrusions. Then we go to " Nausicaa " and suddenly we have this marmalady voice of Gerty's consciousness (a kind of mass-media voice), then we move into the Bloom passages, then we're into a totally different realm when we enter " Oxen ". The voices of the past come at us from various directions, conveying a kind of minimum reality, representing a minimal statement of experience in styles which at one time we would have supposed to be clear.

83. *Gottfried.* – If, as I suggest, one postulates a narrative which, from the very opening chapters, is characterized by intentional manipulation, by a syntactic scrambling, mixing and alternating the order of phrases and parts of speech, such a narrative is even more noticeable in the later chapters, where linguistic patterns become increasingly evident and language insists more strongly on its presence in

the text *as language*. Moreover, if such syntactic alternation of phrases results in a combination of character and narrator, of inner world and outer worlds of the novel, what could more clearly be the epitome of such narrative than " Circe ", where the psychologies of the characters are brought out into the events of the evening.

In the later chapters, thus, the narrative does not decline, nor change, it only becomes more clearly what it was : demonstrating its nature as manipulated language more forcefully. The characters do not disappear, but rather are more closely interwoven into the linguistic texture which expresses them.

The opening of " Circe ", seemingly a transition from demonstrative narrative to dramatic form, still demonstrates the basic element of Joyce's narration : a sentence such as " Round Rabaiotti's halted ice gondola stunted men and women squabble ", or " From drains, clefts, cesspools, middens arise on all sides stagnant fumes " clearly evidence the characteristic manipulations of the order of words ; subjects and predicates are reversed even within the " stage directions " of the chapter. The patterns of language which are being manipulated are made increasingly evident in the later chapters as language asserts its presence in the text. Both " Circe " and " Ithaca " abound in sentences patently stressing such patterns : " Was then she him you us since knew ? " (" Circe ") ; " With thought of aught he sought though frought with naught " (" Ithaca "). The question and answer catechism of " Ithaca " continues and fosters the fundamental linguistic features of Joycean narrative. There are successive sentences within the same series of questions, some of which seek to undo the order of syntax, and others which insist on that order :

> " What suggested scene was then constructed by Stephen ? Solitary hotel in mountain pass. Autumn. Twilight. Fire lit. In dark corner young man seated. Young woman enters. Restless. Solitary. She sits.
>
> What suggested scene was then reconstructed by Bloom ? The Queen's Hotel, Ennis, County Clare, where Rudolph Bloom (Rudolf Virag) died on the evening of 27 June 1886, at some hour unstated, in consequence of an overdose of monkshood (aconite) selfadministered... " (684).

Both show the language of narration being altered and transformed.

Moreover, such scrambling of syntax and insistence on the presence of language *per se* succeeds in combining character and narrator, inner world and outer, to the point that it is syntactically as well as psychologically feasible for Stephen and Bloom to interchange phrases : for example, where Bloom calls out against the Nymph in Stephen's magical incantation : " Holy Nebrakada " (553), or Molly calls to her camel in the same word " Nebrakada ! Feminimum " (440). Character has not subsided ; rather language, character's essence in all fiction, has come to the fore.

84. *Benstock.* – What do we do with the information about how many lovers Molly Bloom has had, with the facts about the agency fire, with the scene that Stephen relates about the hotel room (and in the next question Bloom thinks

about the hotel room in which his father died). How do we know what sort of tone is set here – and is there a consistency ? If so, how does it cut ?

85. *Gottfried.* – Joyce is able to get somebody interested in at least an alternate version of the famous epic with which this novel shares a correspondence of events – i.e., Homer's *Odyssey* where Penelope takes lovers. Why can't he simply have Molly make known the list of her past lovers ? The method he chooses, indirect as it is, still is consistent with the naturalistic core of the text. We get too much information, too many facts, we don't know how the perspective is skewered (we can guess, knowing Bloom's predisposition, but such speculation remains merely speculative). But in sorting out the question of narrative techniques and narrative *levels* we musn't forget the allusive structure of this work.

86. *Hayman.* – We really haven't touched on that at all. And, of course, the allusive levels are a very important aspect of the book because they underlie so much of what is going on. They help direct the machinery of the narration. But at the same time, earlier critics overdid that aspect of it, and I think all of us have the tendency to shy away from what was so extremely exaggerated by critics like Gilbert, but we should probably keep the allusive strain in mind. The allusive structure gives a kind of density to the novel and adds to our amusement, if you will. And, of course, when you talk about Penelope you are really talking about two Penelopes. At one point in his notes Joyce writes that Ulysses was lucky, Penelope was unfaithful. And it is the unfaithful Penelope who is projected for us in this list in " Ithaca ", whereas the faithful Penelope occupies our minds. She is the one who dominates our image of the *Odyssey*.

87. *Hagopian.* – It is fashionable to regard literary works as a sort of stimuli-producing machine where turning the page is like turning the crank on a machine that bombards you with stimuli. You respond with free associations of all kinds – some are associations from literary history, including names of previous works, etc., all of which have a mystical, literary, and verbal power to lull you but which ultimately are just nonsense. I like the description of this chapter which emphasizes that the complex phenomena which evolve, and the shifting perceptions which render experience, ultimately do define a specific experience that can be read, understood, and felt. This chapter, written in a strange catechism technique, does render human experience which does become conceivable when you stop experiencing the technique and learn the particular words – i.e., how to read it, to make it translusive, to read *through* it. But such an explanation still doesn't answer the question : why *this* technique ? Perhaps the answer is that this technique shows us the absurdity of trying to understand human experience by accumulating lots of facts – for instance, the list of Molly's lovers. It doesn't matter how many she's had. Her infidelity is a fact of the novel – it is a functional, psychological chart of experience that we know about. How many lovers she has had in the past, where, and when are basically incidental and extraneous to this novel.

88. *Seidel.* – I don't think it is necessary to make a decision like that. The chapter just gives psychological information, as John Hagopian pointed out, information about how " human lives work ". But it also gives us information about how the book is made, it moves from the naturalistic level to something else (I don't want to call it a " symbolistic " level because that is too simple). But the novel does reflect on what it does – in many complex ways.

89. *Mitchell.* – We might add one thing that Joyce did say about the setting of the chapter – i.e., that he was placing Stephen and Bloom in a cosmological context really, showing them in their proper perspective with the stars, planets, and so forth. And this might help to answer the queston of why he employs this pseudo-scientific technique. This is not to say that science can answer all the questions – or provide the answers to these questions, but simply to show that there is a realm – a realm of physical laws, the movements of planets, and so forth – to which Bloom and Stephen are related. Joyce felt that he was showing this, among other things, in this episode. The other side of the point is that there is a story being told in this chapter, but it is being told through questions and answers – such a technique in fiction is *new*.

90. *Hayman.* – We come closest here to a very ordinary kind of narrative. We come closest to the point where we are really being told by a series of actions a story that is rendered in a super-objective voice.

Audience. – I'm surprised to find myself agreeing with Dr. Hagopian. We have a " technique " here which really isn't scientific at all – it may be a parody of science. It does suggest that the information which the traditional narrative has always tended to give in plenty is not sufficient for certain kinds of human experience – and one of the ways you see this is through " Ithaca " which is followed by " Penelope " whose narrative is subjective and self-centered. This still doesn't answer the question of why so *much* information is thrown at us, pell-mell in " Ithaca ".

91. *Benstock.* – In organizing this panel, I had hoped that we might succeed in asking a number of questions that seem relevant to a study of narrative technique in *Ulysses*. While we certainly have provided no hard-and-fast rules for reading the book successfully, nor have we solved many of the innumerable difficulties provided by the narrative, I think we have succeeded in asking some relevant and pointed questions. I deliberately chose panel members who represent different critical perspectives on *Ulysses* and whose opinions on the work were guaranteed to be controversial – in arousing a certain degree of enthusiastic discussion we have also been successful. As for those questions that still nag – i.e., why is so much information thrown at the reader in Ithaca ? ; who controls the Circean hallucination ; what is stream of consciousness and what is not in this novel ? – we clearly need to probe the narrative further and perhaps work toward developing a critical vocabulary, as Breon Mitchell mentioned this

morning and as Fritz Senn has long advocated, that will allow us to describe more accurately narrative functions in *Ulysses*.

*
* *

Passages from Ulysses for panel on narrative techniques (1961 Random House).

Page 28 :

Across the page the symbols moved in grave morrice, in the mummery of their letters, wearing quaint caps of squares and cubes. Give hands, traverse, bow to partner : so : imps of fancy of the Moors. Gone too from the world, Averroes and Moses Maimonides, dark men in mien and movement, flashing in their mocking mirrors the obscure soul of the world, a darkness shining in brightness which brightness could not comprehend.

     — Do you understand now ? Can you work the second for yourself ?

     — Yes, sir.

In long shady strokes Sargent copied the data. Waiting always for a word of help his hand moved faithfully the unsteady symbols, a faint hue of shame flickering behind his dull skin. *Amor matris :* subjective and objective genitive. With her weak blood and wheysour milk she had fed him and hid from sight of others his swaddling bands.

Like him was I, these sloping shoulders, this gracelessness. My childhood bends beside me. Too far for me to lay a hand there once or lightly. Mine is far and his secret as our eyes. Secrets, silent, stony sit in the dark palaces of both our hearts : secrets weary of their tyranny : tyrants willing to be dethroned.

The sum was done.

Page 65 :

The sluggish cream wound curdling spirals through her tea. Better remind her of the word : metempsychosis. An example would be better. An example ?

The bath of the Nymph over the bed. Given away with the Easter number of *Photo Bits :* Splendid masterpiece in art colours. Tea before you put milk in. Not unlike her with her hair down : slimmer. Three and six I gave for the frame. She said it would look nice over the bed. Naked nymphs : Greece : and for instance all the people that lived then.

He turned the pages back.

     — Metempsychosis, he said, is what the ancient Greeks called it. They used to believe you could be changed into an animal or a tree, for instance. What they called nymphs, for example.

Her spoon ceased to stir up the sugar. She gazed straight before her, inhaling through her arched nostrils.

     — There's a smell of burn, she said. Did you leave anything on the fire ?

     — The kidney ! he cried suddenly.

He fitted the book roughly into his inner pocket and, stubbing his toes against the broken commode, hurried out towards the smell, stepping hastily down the stairs with a flurried stork's legs. Pungent smoke shot up in an angry jet from a side of the pan. By prodding a prong of the fork under the kidney he detached it and turned it turtle on its back. Only a little burned. He tossed it off the pan on to a plate and let the scanty brown gravy trickle over it.

Page 429 :

The Mabbot street entrance of nighttown, before which stretches an uncobbled tramsiding set with skeleton tracks, red and green will-o'-the-wisps and danger signals. Rows of flimsy houses with gaping doors. Rare lamps with faint rainbow fans. Round Rabaiotti's halted ice gondola stunted men and women squabble. They grab wafers between which are wedged lumps of coal and copper snow. Sucking, they scatter slowly. Children. The swancomb of the gondola, highreared, forges on through the murk, white and blue under a lighthouse. Whistles call and answer.

The Calls

Wait, my love, and I'll be with you.

The Answers

Round behind the stable.

(A deafmute idiot with goggle eyes, his shapeless mouth dribbling, jerks past, shaken in Saint Vitus' dance. A chain of children's hands imprisons him).

Page 684-85 :

What suggested scene was then constructed by Stephen ?

Solitary hotel in mountain pass. Autumn. Twilight. Fire lit. In dark corner young man seated. Young woman enters. Restless. Solitary. She sits. She goes to window. She stands. She sits. Twilight. She thinks. On solitary hotel paper she writes. She thinks. She writes. She sighs. Wheels and hoofs. She hurries out. He comes from his dark corner. He seizes solitary paper. He holds it toward fire. Twilight. He reads. Solitary.

What ?

In sloping, upright and backhand : Queen's hotel, Queen's hotel, Queen's Ho...

What suggested scene was then reconstructed by Bloom ?

The Queen's Hotel, Ennis, County Clare, where Rudolph Bloom (Rudolph Virag) died on the evening of the 27 June 1886, at some hour unstated, in consequence of an overdose of monkshood (aconite) selfadministered in the form of a neuralgic liniment, composed of 2 parts of aconite liniment to 1 of chloroform liniment (purchased by him at 10:20 a.m. on the morning of 27 June 1886 at the medical hall of Francis Dennehy, 17 Church street, Ennis) after having, though not in consequence of having, purchased at 3:15 p.m. on the afternoon of 27 June 1886 a new boater straw hat, extra smart (after having, though not in consequence of having, purchased at the hour and in the place aforesaid, the toxin aforesaid), at the general drapery store of James Cullen, 4 Main Street, Ennis.

" A Portrait of the Artist " :
Structure and Theme
(A summary of the panel)

A Portrait of the Artist
as a Young Man :
Syntax and Style

Into the first version of his autobiographical novel, *Stephen Hero,* Joyce " packed incident after thinly disguised incident from real life " (1). Before that he had written a short sketch of his youth entitled *A Portrait of the Artist.* In the final version *A Portrait of the Artist as a Young Man* he conveyed his ideas of the developing artist. It was " an artistic unity for which *A Portrait of the Artist* and *Stephen Hero* are only preliminary sketches " (2). To gain the artistic unity of the novel Joyce needed a new technique both in structure and style. He had to turn from objective to subjective narration. To succeed in this task he introduced a new technique to capture " the individuating rhythm " of that " fluid succession of presents " which constitute the past. In Joyce's production *A Portrait of the Artist as a Young Man* may be seen as a transition from the often naturalistic *Dubliners* to *Ulysses,* in which Joyce explored the stream of consciousness technique thoroughly.

A Portrait of the Artist as a Young Man represents the genre of " Bildungsroman " in which the development of the protagonist is revealed through his mental experience, from the inside and through a technique which, in many passages, can be called a stream-of-consciousness technique, not always direct interior monologue, but direct.

To work out the structure based on very subjective revelations demands a special and varied use of syntax and style. For Joyce, a born linguist, language was a sixth sense, the machinery through which the human organism revealed its inner processes.

---

(1) Beja, Morris, *James Joyce, A Portrait of the Artist as a Young Man, A Casebook,* London, 1973, p. 19.
(2) Schutte, William M., *Twentieth Century Interpretations of A Portrait of the Artist as a Young Man,* New Jersey, 1968, p. 6.

Joyce wanted to show *what* Stephen apprehends at any point in his career and *how* he apprehends (3).

I shall follow the technique used in different chapters paying attention to the syntactic features. Thus my approach is linguistic, rather than literary. For instance, in Chapter 1 Stephen's childhood is described in such linguistic structures as correspond to Stephen's age. In the second chapter dealing with Stephen's adolescence his inner subjective world is conveyed with more subtly designed insight than in the first chapter. In the third chapter language plays an important role in Father Arnall's sermons " Masterpieces of oratory ", in which the rhetorical resources of language are exploited to the full (4). Stephen's reactions to the terrifying vision of damnation aroused by the sermons are expressed by his mental flux of associations in a way that comes very near to interior monologue.

The narrative method approaching the stream-of-consciousness technique is here carried further than in the previous chapters. The flux of associations is accompanied with the breaking away from normal syntax resulting in that kind of interior monologue to be found in *Ulysses*. The use of the stream-of-consciousness technique in its " purest " form (from the technical point of view) is characteristic of the final, diary section of the novel, in which Stephen is recording his thoughts after his decision to go abroad, in exile.

Liisa DAHL
University of Turku

The Green Rose :
Image as Structure
in A Portrait of the Artist as a Young Man

It is obvious that Joyce's novels are not " written " in the usual sense ; rather, they are constructed according to esthetic principles preached by Stephen in *Portrait* and practised by Joyce there and elsewhere : wholeness, harmony, and radiance. Harmony, or the relationship of part to part, bears most directly on structure in *Portrait*. I am particularly interested in the way in which recurring images form a part of this structure, and, more specifically, in how one such image, the green rose, pervasively and non-discursively expresses the persistent clashes between Stephen's inner life and his outer circumstances.

At the begining of *Portrait*, Stephen as a young child transforms the red rose of the song into a green rose, and the fundamental conflict between the green of his imagination and the red of external reality is thus initiated, a conflict which

---

(3) Routh, H.V., *English Literature and Ideas in the Twentieth Century ; An Inquiry into Present Difficulties and Future Prospects*, London, 1948, p. 169.
(4) Sucksmith, Harvey Peter, *James Joyce : A Portrait of the Artist as Young Man*, London, 1973, p. 44.

continues in significant variations throughout the novel. There are other central, recurring and reflexive images which operate in the same fashion, and which collectively form an important structural element of the novel.

Robert RYF
Occidental College

A Portrait and Vico Reconsidered

Joyce's concept of the epiphany and its use in *Dubliners* is closely akin to his concept of the Viconian recorso, a moment – a period – when old things fall apart, disintegrate, and when with eyes burning " with anguish and anger " one sees the vain illusions of one's life laid bare and there is nowhere to go, except phoenix-like to be reborn. The " shaft of shivery " and " cloudclap " in *Finnegans Wake* metaphorically serve the same purpose as do " time's livid final flame, the shattered glass and toppling masonry " of *Ulysses*. In writing in *Portrait* about Stephen's studies of Aristotle and Aquinas, Joyce says : " His thinking was a dusk of doubt and selfmistrust lit up at moments by the lightnings of intuition, but lightnings of so clear a splendour that in those moments the world perished about his feet as if it had been fireconsumed " (117).

The function of the recorso, of the flash of lightning, in the substructure of *Portrait* will be the subject of this paper. In maturing as an artist Joyce began to see radical discontinuity as a creative stylistic device to produce not only the insights of his characters but to stimulate those of his readers and himself. This radical discontinuity began to function as the very fabric of his craft at the same time that he was enunciating the credo that only when the old order has been reduced to ashes can new life arise. By contrast, the epiphany of *Dubliners* tends to stress the moments of insight and the disintegration of the old ways, not, as with the recorso, the emergence ot new ones as well.

Margaret CHURCH
Purdue University

The non-age of Joyce :
A re-examination
of some critical truths

The basic purpose of our meeting today, beyond the pleasures of Paris and springtime, is to investigate anew the enduring import of James Joyce, the greatest master in what may be the greatest of literary epochs. His reputation, more than three decades after his death, is ever-increasing : the Modernist era as we view it today might as accurately be called the Age of Joyce. But we may need to question how enduring his actual influence has been : most critics agree that Modernism is now dead, that we are living in a new, transitional period labelled (let us hope temporarily) Post-Modernism. The implications of this change for Joycean studies are quite considerable, I believe, relating both to Joyce's effect on his own time and to influence on this later one : what we might term, as an entity, Joyce's aura, a repository of possibilities which other writers may choose to pursue or to reject but which they cannot simply ignore. In the expanding dialogue involving Modernism and Post-Modernism, between the art of a past generation and those who would deny the old out of hand, it seems to me to be increasingly important to determine what models Joyce actually did provide for his contemporaries and successors and what uses they have made of these models. To do so entails the re-examination of many long accepted critical truths about Joyce and his work ; it necessitates as well an overview of the Modernist movement and some sense at least of the newly developing post-Modern sensibility. A tentative step in this uncertain direction is the task which I envisage for our panel today.

It is a difficult task. We must determine at the start whether Joyce, unmistakably the dominant figure of his age, is in fact its literary exemplar ; there are many stories of the awe in which Joyce was held by his contemporaries, but specific cases of influence may be more difficult to prove. (The ambiguous case of Faulkner comes most readily to mind.) We must determine as well the converse issue, whether the movement into this new age, if such it is, represents a repudiation of Joyce's example ; certain contemporary writers specifically abjure the continuing import of this work, yet we may discover his traces even in their work. (Robbe-Grillet is the most obvious illustration of this point.) The issue of models − of technique and of outlook − is equally important, although its individual aspects may appear more narrow. We may wonder, for instance, whether Joyce's use of point of view and his handing of time are as revolutionary and instructive as they have seemed − is the stream of consciousness both illustrative of the Modernist sensibility and a formative force in its creation ? Are *Ulysses* and *Finnegans Wake* quite as encyclopedic as we have thought − encompassing virtually all the knowledge and values of their time − and how representative are they of contemporary attitudes ? (Compare Proust and Mann ; compare Pynchon and Gaddis.) What use does Joyce make of the mythic method − reflecting his attitudes toward the standards of his time and toward those of the past − and what does this imply for his work and for those who follow in his path ? (Kazantzakis and Broch, Coover and Barthe seem pertinent here.) Finally, what is Joyce's view of humanist survival in a world of diminishing potential − is he closer to Bloom or to Stephen ? − and to what is this worldview characteristic of either age ? Such issues go to the heart of both Modernist and post-Modernist areas : to this extent, at least, Joyce remains indisputably the central literary figure of the twentieth century.

In England, however, Joyce seems to have had no enduring influence at all. Judging from English fiction today − aside from occasional echoes in the works of such writers as Burgess and Powell − it would seem that the Modernist era had never occurred. The contemporary novelists and critics of England look not to Joyce and to Woolf for their models but to Dickens and Trollope and Fielding. Their subject matter is contemporary, to be sure, but in outlook and technique they are not post-Modern but pre-. The New Victorians we might more appropriately name them.

Writers on the Continent have been more observant, endeavoring to expand the insights of Joyce and his contemporaries and to develop from them a sensibility suited to a new generation ; Simon, Grass, Johnson, Vassilikós, Bassani and Claude Mauriac are but a few of those whose work shows the continued imprint of the Modernists. Their work is significant in itself ; it is not merely a latter-day imitation of modernist modes. Yet one may sometimes feel that some of these novels pay too much homage to the lesson of Joyce, that too little new ground has been broken in imitation of Joyce. Michel Butor is one who has felt this way and who has attempted to break out of these bonds and to create entirely new forms of fiction. We admire his daring and inventiveness, yet we also note that his latest, post-Modernist books are much less compelling in human terms than the early novels written under the influence of Joyce. Is it impossible then to learn from the master's example without also denying him ? Is there no positive means of incorporating still valid Modernist perceptions in new fictional forms ?

This quandary is one that many North American novelists have obviously experienced. Theirs is a fiction still very much in transition. A decade ago, we might have argued convincingly that Modernism was more enduring in the United States − Bellow and a few others aside − than it was in England. But recent efforts have shown more and more traces of Joyce, utilizing in highly individualistic ways Joycean techniques in narration, in the development of myth, in the elaboration of encyclopedic forms, dealing with increasing directness with Joycean attitudes and themes. But it is still too early to be certain of their ultimate goals : do they act in emulation of Joyce ? in conscious adaptation of this example ? or is theirs a sophisticated, Joycean means of progressing beyond, even of repudiating Joyce ? It may take another decade before we − novelists as well as critics − can answer these questions definitively.

But there is a current solution, I believe ; it is to be found in the fiction of Latin America, to my mind the most exciting and challenging fiction being created today. This is neither *Modernismo* reborn nor Modernism a generation late, but a literature that builds upon the Modernist advances in style and technique, that learns from the Modernist insights into the nature of man and his limited life and that adds to them an experience and attitude drawn from the lifestyle of a new continent. One example of this union is *Mulatta,* by Miguel Angel Asturias, an hallucinatory wedding of Jungian and Guatemalan mythology, a sort of *Finnegans Wake* as dreamed by a direct descendant of the ancient Mayans. Perhaps the two finest novels since *Finnegans Wake* are similarly from Latin America : Carlos Fuentes' *The Death of Artemio Cruz* and *One Hundred Years of Solitude,* by Gabriel García Márquez. Such works transcend local history ; by building on the example of Joyce and his contemporaries, they are able to create a fabulous new growth, a new series of metaphors from which to view man in a changing yet unchanged world. They suggest very convincingly that the aura of Joyce remains vital today, that novelists as well as critics have much to learn yet from his example. Our task may thus be less historical and more alive than it had previously seemed. And there may be more of a role for Joyceans in it than we might have thought.

Morton P. Levitt
Temple University.

(Summary) :

Is Joyce still a topical literary phenomenon or does his work belong to one particular moment in literary history, that of modernism ? *Ulysses* is a pivot for all modernist procedure, and the attention payed to Joyce by post-modern writers is therefore of particular interest. For post-modern means more freedom, openness, improvisation ; on principle, a post-modern work does not aspire to the autonomy and hermeticism characteristic of the symbolist inheritance of which Joyce is a superior model.

Authors in national literatures that have only more recently begun to express a modern sensibility have consciously learned from Joyce, especially in their structuring of fiction through a deliberate use of thematic leit-motifs, etc. On the other hand, the modernist experiment continues to be felt today, though − with some exceptions − it relies less on the consistency of method than Joyce's generation did. If at one time it was Joyce's recreation of the working of consciousness that was of central interest, in the last twenty years the dominant influence has been in the creative use of language as a way of structuring personal vision and in pastiche and parody. Also, it is through the peculiar use of language that the image of man on a totality of objects has found its most impressive crystallization. We have been witnessing a shift of interest from the stream of consciousness, from an analogy with the impressionist method, if we like, towards *a)* a view of the anthropological significance of the non-historical unity between the contemporary and the constant mythical aspects of human behaviour, and *b)* towards the techniques tending towards abstraction, precise enumeration, and description.

Ivo VIDAN,
University of Zagreb.

(Summary) :

My first assumption is that Joyce was not basically and permanently influenced by any single movement, school, epoch, person, or theory. He was no romantic, no impressionist, naturalist, symbolist, surrealist, or expressionist and no follower of any other -ism.

But on the other hand there is a basic intention in his works which links him to most of the -isms that he has been labelled with. This intention is introspection and its representation. We all know Stephen's statement : " ...to forge in the smithy of my soul the uncreated conscience of my race ". This statement implies the two main aspects of this intention, the personal one and the social one, i.e. the intra-personal experience and change on one hand and the inter-personal experience and change on the other.

So my second assumption is that Joyce stands in the very old mystical tradition. And when I say mystical and mysticism I mean it in the broadest sense of the term. I mean the very old introspective experience of the unity of God, the human soul and the world.

It is the very attempt to represent the structure of the soul or the functioning of consciousness or the complementary of intra- and inter-personal experience which provides the implied message of Joyce's works : it is the experience of eternal change, of the interrelation of all phenomena, of the coincidence of contraries, the experience of the complementarity of I and world, i.e. the experience of the I as always broken open – a picture which is derived from the German word *" aufbrechen "* which means to break open, to burst open, to set out.

This seems to be the basis of Joyce's psycho-literary experiments and the results of these experiments show a definitive similarity to mystical, heretical, and schizophrenic structures of experience or expression. The tendency of Joyce's experiments is antidogmatic, arational, aperspective, and deranged. But being anti, it never loses its bearing upon the dogmatic, the rational, the perspective, the normal.

So I think if there is an influence of Joyce on other authors or vice versa it lies mainly in these results of the introspective experience, it lies in the conviction that every artist has to find his own new way of creative introspection, of intra and interpersonal experience and change.

Norbert C. SCHMUHL,
Waldkirch.

Joyce and Brancusi

The Brancusi Portrait

(What it meant to Joyce).

In the interval before the book was published, Joyce was able to make a relevant addition. The first of the fragments, *The Mookse and the Gripes,* is told in terms of Church history and practice. Before he wrote it, he made a list of words that would fit the ecclesiastical context. Among these, he put " constantinently ", a reference to the emperor who established Christianity as the official Roman religion. However, in 1927, when the fable appeared in *transition,* he had not yet found a way in which to do it, a way in which to give the multiplicity of levels which the method of his work required. When the drawing was made by Constantin Brancusi, the word acquired a new meaning. And, by good fortune, there was a passage in *transition* to which this meaning was appropriate.

The Mookse is Shaun, a devotee of Space. The Gripes is Shem, a devotee of Time and Change. In the fable, the Gripes (or Grapes) turns into a raisin. There was a reference in *transition* to the " shapewrecked Gripes ". Now – two years later – it could serve as description of the *Portrait of Joyce.* In this context, " constaninently " would mean 'in the manner of Brancusi'. It would now have the additional level.

" My building space is always to let to men, the Mookse concluded ". Then a new sentence. " (What a crammer for the shapewrecked Gripes !) ". This in *transition.* In the new version, Joyce made several changes, two of which concern us. Brancusi, as a sculptor – or, in this case, the man who made the *Portrait* – is a devotee of Space. For the purpose, limited purpose, of this passage, he is a Mookse. Joyce now added the word " constantinently ". And to make sure that we see it is related to the Gripes, he united what had originally been two separate sentences. After the Mookse's words, the passage now reads, " constantinently concludded *(sic)* " and – as a part of the same sentence – " (what a crammer for the shapewrecked Gripes !) ". Notice that the word " concluded ", which in *transition* was equivalent to " said ", has acquired the additional suggestion that the Mookse (Constantin Brancusi) has brought out as an effect the drawing of the Joyce-like Gripes.

Joyce's taste in art tended to the conventional. While his own went increasingly in areas that hitherto were unexplored, where others were concerned, he stuck to what he knew and understood when he was in Dublin.

In July, he wrote to Valery Larbaud, " I hope that you ... like the edition. What do you think of ... Brancusi's whirligig ? ".

He had written to Miss Weaver about the making of the *Portrait*. " I got on well with Brancusi ... But I wish he or Antheil, say, would be as explicit as I try to be when people ask me : And what's this here, Guvnor ? ".

What he saw was a " wrecked " face, a " whirligag ", a spiral that was put upon the page without any rationale or explanation.

However, there is reason to believe that, a few years later, the writer had occasion to reconsider the *Portrait* and, in so doing, to impose a meaning or − perhaps − a constellation of meanings.

In the Musée National d'Art Moderne − (the contents of Brancusi's studio were willed to the nation) − there is another version of the *Portrait of Joyce*. It was executed in ink with a brush in a gently wavering line. The disposition of the spiral and the three vertical lines is almost exactly that of the familiar *Portrait*. But dispersed around it and in evident relation to the graphic elements are several groups of letters, clearly in Brancusi's hand, also executed by brush.

At the upper left, over the vertical line, we see a capital A, followed by a small *a* − a symbol between them. Over the spiral and somewhat to the right, we find O.E.P., the symbol, O.S.P. Between the spiral and the top of the line on the right, we find a capital *M*. Under this line, we have O.R.F., symbol, O.E.P.

One would think that all parts of this drawing were made at the same time. Yet the lines and spiral have been drawn in a rather free-hand fashion ; while, by contrast, the letters are ranged with orderly precision. It may be that this is the sketch, the initial idea, for the final version that he made for the photographer or printer. If so, it stayed in Brancusi's studio : then for some reason he added the letters. The alternative is that here is a rough copy of the printed version − to *which* he added the letters. Either way, the letters were conceived after the *Portrait* was already in existence. They were added to a drawing which, in plastic terms, was self-sufficient : it needed no additions. A supplement − especially one that is alphabetical − is not characteristic of Brancusi. He tended to subtract. It is James Joyce who, in his second thoughts, tended to amplification. The conviction develops that these letters, though drawn by Brancusi, were there at Joyce's suggestion. If this is the case, they should have a meaning − (though it does not leap to the eye) − which is related to his *Work in Progress*.

In the normal course of events, when there is a mystery, there will be many who offer their solution. It is an accepted thing for someone (in essay or lecture) to make a resumé of the speculations. This is what we're doing. Only − at the present time − all of the speculations are ours.

The symbol is the first of the mystifications. It resembles a small sigma. However, this is not certain. Moreover − if a sigma − we do not see what it is supposed to signify. We suggest that − whatever it may be − it is used as a break between two units. The initials O.E.P. are a single unit. So are O.S.P. The symbol is a stop, a point of demarcation. This would be the case with the O.R.F. and the O.E.P. So, too, with the *A* and *a.*

What do the letters mean ? Take the *A* and *a.* We have mentioned *391,* the first issues of which were published in Zurich in 1917, a time when Joyce was there. From time to time, Tzara contributed an article about " Monsieur Aa, l'antiphilosophe ". This is spelled as in the drawings.

Travesties, a new play by Tom Stoppard, has some confrontations between Joyce and Tzara. I once asked Budgen whether he or Joyce had known Tristan Tzara or any of the other dadaists in Zurich. He looked down his nose ; then he snorted, " No !! *We* had work to do ". Yet Joyce knew of their activities. Or, at any rate, he did in 1920. In a letter to Stanislaus, he says, " Please contradict the following reports at present in circulation about me ... That I founded in Zurich the dadaist... ".

By this time, both Joyce and *391* had come to Paris. Tzara continued to contribute articles about *Aa.* In 1924, the publication folded. But, in that year, there was another − even better − reason for Joyce to be aware of the anti-philosopher. In the fourth issue of his *Transatlantic Review,* Ford Madox Ford included what he called a Literary Supplement. This had three pieces which were described as " From Work in Progress : by I, James Joyce − by II, Tristan Tzara − by III, Ernest Hemingway ". Tzara's contribution had the title " MONSIEUR Aa L'ANTIPHILOSOPHE ". With the exception of the small *a,* all of the letters in the title are capitals (As in the drawing).

I asked Maria Jolas whether, to her knowledge, Joyce knew Tzara in Paris. She remembered that, one night in a café, the waiter brought a note saying that Tzara who was present wondered if M. Joyce would be willing to meet him. For whatever reason, he declined to do so. It is possible they met on some later occasion. But − Mrs. Jolas added − even if they did not meet, Joyce would have known about him. He picked up knowledge through his pores *(See note p. 75).*

For any of these reasons − in any of these fashions − he may have learned about the anti-philosopher. It is hard to prove : hard to disprove. But − having gone this far − we come to a wall. There are places where " dada " as one word or two (that is, " da da "), is mentioned in the *Wake.* Yet, even then, there is no apparent link to the *Portrait of Joyce,* to Tzara or to his creation, Monsieur Aa. If Joyce intended to use this allusion, he either dropped the notion or, if he didn't − (he was a saving man) − it was somehow altered in the process.

Again. There is a drawing in *The Muddest Trick* − the part of Chapter Ten that was in the Crosby booklet. It appeared in *transition* a year before Brancusi made the *Portrait*. The drawing (a Euclidean diagram) consists of two intersecting circles, with a rhombus in the section that they have in common. The drawing has some letters : they designate the points of the rhombus. At the left-hand vertex, a large *A* is followed by a little *alpha*.

The drawing is described as " Views of Dublin ". The Brancusi drawing may have given this a retroactive meaning. If the Brancusi is to be called a portrait − one may say that here is another. The circles are the oversize glasses. They take a 'View of Dublin '. The lozenge or rhombus is a nose on which the glasses rest and over which they peer. Is the *Aa* on the left-hand side of the *Portrait* a reflection of these letters ?

As for the *M* − it is unadorned : no symbol, no period. We have entertained, and rejected, the notion that Brancusi was thinking of a metronome when he made the *Portrait*. Joyce had a different perspective. He had the knowledge of his own intention. To him the booklet dealt with the antinomy of Time and Space. Looking at the drawing, he may have seen a likeness to the instrument. (" Why can't you beat time ? ") M is, *inter alia*, a symbol for a metronome.

This would throw a light on the " Aa ". In a musical context, it could represent *Andante amoroso*. (On p. 116, Joyce compares himself with the writer of the *Song of Songs*.) But in such a context, who is represented by the various initials ?

In the combinations O.E.P., O.S.P., O.R.F., each of the letters is followed by a period. In each group, the first letter is *O*. Does it have an identical meaning ? What of the other letters ?

An important passage in *The Muddest Thick* dealt with Ezra Pound. Another is about St. Patrick. E.P., S.P. − Is there a similar passage about an R.F. ? We have not found it.

The year in which the drawing was made and the *Tales* were published, 1929, also saw the printing of *Our Exagmination. O.* was the symbol Joyce used when speaking of this book. E.P. − Eliot Paul − was one of the contributors. Who is S.P. ? Who is R.F. ? (Roger Fry is mentioned in the *Wake ;* but he does not fit either of the contexts.)

The Muddest Thick was published in *transition* and the *Tales* without the marginal notes that at the present time festoon both of the pages. In 1934, Joyce began to write the first part of the chapter, the section known as *Storiella*. This included working on the margins − both in *Storiella* and *The Muddest Thick*. " Aa " *et al* are similarly placed on both sides of the *Portrait*. We know that Joyce saw Brancusi in 1930. Though we have no witness to a subsequent meeting, it is quite plausible that such meetings occurred. (Though Joyce moved around, his home was often within walking distance of the studio.) It is also possible that Joyce began to make preliminary notes some years before he worked on the first drafts of the marginalia. (This was his practice.) If the letters were added to the *Portrait at the time that he was thinking of these comments (between 1930 and 1934) one would surmise that the letters and the comments are related.*

In this chapter, the sons are schoolboys who are doing their lessons. In *Storiella,* the comments in the left-hand margin are those of Shem. In the right-hand margin, they are Shaun's. Later in the chapter – in *The Muddest Thick* – there are several pages without marginalia. When the comments are resumed, the attribution is reversed. In the rest of the chapter, Shaun has the left-hand phrases. Shem is on the right.

In the letters that begin with *O* there is a similar inversion. These are two lines with an *M* between them. One of the meanings of *M* is middle. O.E.P. is to the left : then it's to the right. Does this reflect the movement of Shem ? Is *M* the middle in which there are no comments ? Is this a model of what will happen in the chapter ? Do the letters form an *X* that foreshadows the shift – the chiasma – Joyce will use in Ten ?

Inversion of opposites is a favorite device of Joyce's. In Chapter X, we get the *visible* example. But there are others – which may throw a light upon it. In the Prank Quean, Shaun and Shem are named Tristopher and Hilary. After forty years, Tristopher becomes a Hilary. Hilary becomes a 'tristan'.

The number of years is meaningful. Man is a cricketer : « his stumps are pulled at eighty ". " The arc of his drive (is) forty. " This is the halfway mark, the middle point – the M. Shaun begins to lose the powers which have made him Shaun. Shem, the (creative) powers which have made him Shem. Without these powers, Hilary becomes like Shaun. Tristopher becomes a Shem.

We have said that the mark between the units may be a little sigma. (Our second choice is a little delta.) Let us now suppose that the M is *Mu.* In Greek – the numerical value of Mu is forty. After M – the changes occur.Shem from left to right. Shaun from right to left.

And yet – why is O.E.P. a Shem ? Why is O.S.P. equivalent to O.R.F. ? Why are they types of Shaun ? Why two separate Shauns and a single Shem ? Why were the letters (whatever they may mean) added to the *Portrait* ? If Joyce wanted a reminder for himself, why did he need to have Brancusi do it ? Once again, the breakthrough – if it is a breakthrough – is no more than partial.

Let us try to answer one of the unanswered questions. Why did he need Brancusi ? He may have thought *Storiella* – too – would be published in a privately printed edition. The *Portrait,* once again, would serve as a frontis-piece ; but in a modulation, an annotated version – " the same anew " – with the addition of the letters.

The notion was discarded. (If he ever had it.) *Storiella* did appear (1937) in a limited edition – without any portrait. Yet the possibility that it may have been considered opens a new byway for speculation.

What is the meaning of the annotations ? On the left – (for the purpose of *Storiella)* – they refer to Shem. On the right, they refer to Shaun. As opposed to Shaun, Joyce is a Shem. Taken by himself – he is HCE : he is Shaun + Shem.

" Aa " − it may be − points up the resemblance to the map or diagram in *The Muddest Thick.* He is the Shem − with the bad eye, with the big glasses. Yet, in spite of this, he is one who sees. He offers a full " View of Dublin ".

" Aa " is perhaps a reference to the character who speaks for Tristan Tzara. " Aa " may reflect James Joyce (Jj) as well as Tt. (*A* is the first letter. *J* is the tenth. *T* is the twentieth. Joyce engages in this kind of numerology.) Notice the importance that Joyce would give to the name of Tristan. Also the association with Zurich and the *Transatlantic Review.* For whatever it is worth, he (Tzara) wore a monocle. Jj sees himself − the side which is Shem − as an anti-philosopher.

Or it may be *Andante amoroso.* It is a tempo. It moves : it flows. On the other side, the side which is Shaun, there is " M " : a metronome which *measures* Time !

On the one side, it is the Song of Solomon. On the other − it is a paradigm. It shows the way the Chapter is organized. It shows what happens when one is forty. (This was Joyce's age when he began the book.)

In the *Wake,* Pound is a form of Shaun. Notably in Chapter Ten : in *The Muddest Thick.* In other places, too. On p. 116, the Book of Solomon's Songs is in opposition to the Book of Ezra − he who is a Scribe. (*E.P.* − we have already suggested − may refer to Pound : he who writes a Guide to Money or Kulchur.)

Any of these may apply. (Some are inconsistent − but many are compatible. These may be there in various combinations.) Or, it may be, all of the things I've said, the resemblances I've urged, are no more than the accident of coincidence. In a list of unrelated items, there will alway be an amount of fortuitous resemblance. And yet − Joyce was concerned with such similarities. He was ingenious in finding − subtle in concealing. If, in this case, he did not do what he usually does, that is still another coincidence.

There is the famous passage " Unslow, malswift... " Joyce took the trouble to write it and, in the *Exagmination,* he had Robert McAlmon give an explication he himself had provided. Then he decided not to use it.

It would seem that here we have another item which he did not use. At this point, however, I am going to suggest another possibility. (If it is not relevant, this will be the greatest coincidence of all !) I will offer the hypothesis that Joyce used these letters − these provisional notes − in the pages of *Finnegans Wake,* the pages of *Storiella.*

This fragment first appeared in *transition 23,* July, 1935. Notice the passage which, in the final text, is on p. 269. " The beggar the maid the bigger the mauler. And the greater the patrarc the griefer the pinch ". In the left-hand margin, we find the following notes :

Undante
umoroso
M. 50-50.

Undante umoroso (large *U* small *u*) is derived from *Andante amoroso*. It keeps the implications of flowing and love − with the further comment that it is funny and not like Dante. Notice the " patrarc ". The allusions to Dante and Petrarch were added to a typescript at the same time.

M. 50-50 reflects the relationship of " mauler " and " maid ". (Each begins with *m*.) *M*. is also the abbreviation for 'marriage' − which presumably is 50-50. Notice, too, on a metronome, 50 is consistent which the tempo of *andante amoroso*.

In the privately-printed *Storiella* and in the *Wake,* there are several changes from the *transition* version. One is another comment below M. 50-50. We have spoken of a little sigma − (possibly a little delta) − of a little alpha, a capital Mu. Now a Greek phrase written in Greek letters.

The Greek words are " *ouk elabon polin* ". Omicron eta pi − the letters that begin the words reflect the O.E.P. which was mentioned twice in the annotated Portrait.

It is a traditional schoolboy joke. (It is the schoolboy chapter.) The sounds are equivalent to the French phrase, " Ou qu'est la bonne Pauline ? " − Where is the maid Pauline ? The maid reflects the one in " beggar the maid ". The meaning of the Greek applies to She. Its translation is " he did not conquer the city ".

The " Aa " was always on the left. " M " and " O.E.P. " were originally on the right. Their message (whatever it may have been) was something solemn − Shaun-like. Now they're on the left. The comment is flippant. All of it applies to Shem.

We do not know how much (if any) of this Joyce had in mind when he had Brancusi drape the alphabetical addenda along the sides of his *Portrait*. We have offered several ideas : yet how can we be sure ? But we do feel, with some measure of confidence, that the letters did experience a metamorphosis. They became the frivolous comments in the margin of *Storiella*.

Nathan HALPER

NOTE : For the record, the incident described on p. 65 concerned André Breton, not Tristan Tzara, whom, to my knowledge, Joyce never met. It was Eugene Jolas who, seeing Breton enter the café where we were dining, suggested the introduction to which Joyce politely demurred.

M. Jolas.

The Brancusi portrait

A summary by Nathan Halper

In 1929, Harry and Caresse Crosby of the Black Sun Press in Paris decided to publish a limited edition of three fragments from Joyce's *Work in Progress*. They wanted a portrait of Joyce – preferably by Picasso – to be the frontispiece. When he refused, they approached Brancusi – who agreed. Joyce and Brancusi had met at a dinner given by John Quinn in 1923, but apparently had made no impression on each other. On the occasion of this portrait, they acted as if meeting for the first time. They took to each other – finding they had much in common – and Joyce subsequently paid other visits to Brancusi's studio.

Brancusi first made a naturalist drawing. Then he was urged " to do also an abstract conception ". Brancusi drew a spiral, with a short and a long vertical line to its left and a short line under its right edge. It was reproduced on a separate sheet tipped into the book *Tales Told of Shaun and Shem*. (This is Brancusi's first " abstract " drawing.)

In their accounts of the sitting, Joyce and Mrs. Crosby refer to the original likeness of Joyce in the singular. But there are three portrait – drawings of Joyce by Brancusi. Were they all done at the same time ? We do not know. We do know that Joyce visited Brancusi twice in 1930. (This is the testimony of the painter Jacques Herold who was working there at the time.) The drawings, in any case, are in three small sheets of varying size ; two are in pencil and one in ink drawn with a brush.

Was the " abstract " portrait drawn immediately after the realistic portrait or at a later moment when Brancusi was alone ? Again, we do not know. But it required some preparation to do the spiral since it is swung with mechanical precision in spite of the fact that the weight of the line varies. Brancusi probably wrapped a string around a dowel and put a pen through a loop at the free end. The vertical lines were drawn along a straight edge. In 1954 Brancusi told Richard Ellmann that the drawing " was a 'Symbol of Joyce' and expressed the *'sens du pousser'* (feeling of thrusting) which he thought a principal characteristic ". Ordinarily the spiral is a design rendered on a flat surface, as in the present case, and is seen as centrifugal or centripetal rather than as thrusting. But surely factors other than this reading of it influenced Brancusi's choice of the motif. Early in 1926, while in New York for the first time, Brancusi visited Alfred Stieglitz at the Little Gallery. On the walls during Brancusi's visit, there was an exhibition of work by Arthur Dove that included several assemblages composed of diverse materials. Only a few months before, in the same gallery, Dove had exhibited his *Portrait of Stieglitz,* a work whose most noticeable feature was a large steel spring. The *Portrait* is not listed as being in the 1926 exhibition, but it is very likely that

Stieglitz showed it leaning against the gallery wall, as was his custom to do, and that Brancusi saw it.

But both Dove and Brancusi would have known of other earlier spirals. Intermittently, from 1917 to 1924, Francis Picabia published a little magazine called *391,* the title being a play on the magazine *291* which had been published by Stieglitz. (At this point Geist gives a lot of examples of springs or spirals in *391* and elsewhere. He points out that Brancusi was on friendly terms with Picabia, Duchamp and others who employed this motif.) By the mid-1920's the spiral seems to have become an emblem of modernism. Indeed, it is the first motif to appear in Adolfo Best-Maugard's book, *A Primer of Modern Design,* published in 1926.

If Brancusi told Ellmann that his spiral was a " Symbol of James Joyce " which expressed a characteristic of the writer, another view of the drawing is recorded by Oscar Chelimsky, an American painter who had a studio opposite Brancusi's in this period. He reports that it was with " rather a puzzled air " that Brancusi recounted his relations with Joyce. First he drew a realistic portrait. " I realized at this point that he wanted somethings totally different from what I had in mind, so I made a few geometric scrawls on paper, called it *Portrait of James Joyce,* and off he went content ". The Ellmann and Chelimsky versions of the origin of the drawing are clearly at variance with each other. It was a work whose significance for Brancusi changed according to his moods.

In spite of both versions of the origin – as reflecting Joyce's *"sens du pousser"* or as being " a few geometric scrawls " – it is possible that it is a representation of certain visible Joycean features. It may be seen as a close-up view of the writer : the long line is the nose, the short line at the right marking the edge of the face, and the spiral representing the thick lens which Joyce had to wear over his near-blind left eye. This kind of stylization is encountered in modern caricature, and provides us with a much more likely reason for the drawing's existence than that Brancusi made the drawing out of whole cloth. It can be shown that his seeming abstractions, except for *Endless Column,* derive from an objective reality – from a living creature or an artistic representation of one.

Brancusi almost never made a sculpture from his drawings, yet he translated his Symbol of James Joyce into sculptural terms by placing a spiral of wire in the center of a shallow cone of paper. This fragile object was made at the time he was seeing Joyce – about 1930 – and was photographed hanging on the wall of the studio near the the fireplace. It has disappeared. Among Brancusi's effects, willed with the other products of this studio to the French nation, there was found a mystifying version of the drawing reproduced in *Tales Told of Shaun and Shem.* It is done with brush and ink on cheap paper which has turned brown. (It was found torn and has been restored. Nathan Halper will explore the problems it poses.)

(At this point, there was a pause for questions. One of these was whether the drawing showed the influence of the *Book of Kells.* Geist emphatically answered that it *certainly* did not ! He is much upset because he tells me that a publication of the Musée Moderne quotes him as saying that it did. He feels that somehow this should be set straight).

There was also a discussion of the possible resemblance of the drawing to that of a sort of metronome. The booklet ends with the words " ... why can't you beat time ? " Brancusi may have used this as a theme of his " abstract " drawing. The spiral is the spring ; the long vertical line is the moving rod. Geist thought this was not likely. From his knowledge of the other, he does not believe that Brancusi would have looked at the manuscript − even if they would have brought the proofs. In the accounts of Joyce or Mrs. Crosby, there is no statement that he may have done so. However, Joyce − in due course − may have seen the resemblance. (See Nathan Halper's lecture.)

Sidney GEIST

Joyce's Corpus as Word-Machine

What I had in mind when I proposed the topic, " Joyce's Corpus as Word-Machine ", and what occurred were two different things. I had supposed there would be a four-day workshop, following an initial panel presentation, allowing for a categorizing of sub-topics and thus interchange among attenders of the sessions. Although it seemed, at times, to turn into a contest among speakers to say what they came to say and to hell with listening and responding, what did happen, in the single hour and a half allotted, was perhaps indicative of the peculiar kind of scholarship elicited by *Finnegans Wake*. Each miner of the text takes suspicious note of the cumulative discoveries of others, grudgingly acknowledges his debts − which, by this time, are tremendous indeed − and goes off to his own corner to fondle the bright gems that are going to outshine all other minings and astound the world once they are strung in a coherent *catena*. But, after all, the various " central theories " pile up as additional peripheries (1).

The " Proposal for Workshop " that I submitted to the symposium planners and then, later, distributed to the panel members, will begin the summary of the session's proceedings. Each of the panelists tried, at the start, to respond to the distributed comments ; however, because of the unexpected limitations of time and the consequent strictures imposed by my opening instructions, an inordinate amount of attention was given to the connotations of the word, " machine ", and to the consideration of the term " organic " as a possible alternative. I shall include, in Section I, most of the transcription of the taping of these opening salvos, to show how the controversy was shaped.

Consideration of the selected passage (FW 185.27-186.8) that was supposed to follow the initial presentations and responses of the panelists turned into pretty much of a freeforall, during which panel and audience alike tried to promote particular modes of reading the *Wake* that were, at present, guiding exclusive studies. In Section II, instead of presenting a blow-by-blow transcription in its sequential confusion, I shall try to select, condense, and gather into separate clusters a few of the subjects that didn't die in isolated monologues.

---

(1) See " The James Joyce Industry : A Reassessment ", *Yeats, Joyce and Beckett*, eds., Kathleen McGrory and John Unterecker (Bucknell University Press, 1976), 126-130, where Bernard Benstock reiterates skepticism about any eventual piecing together of the full " mosaic " of *Finnegans Wake*.

When this session ended, I asked myself if anything at all had been accomplished. Now that I have wrestled with the monster-tape, I see that chaos does, inevitably, shape itself, even though the world created is never the expected One.

Proposal for Workshop : Joyce's Corpus as Word-Machine.

I'd like to use Finnegans Wake 185.27-186.8 as the passage of departure, but, rather than limit the discussions to one work, I want to examine the *corpus* as Joyce's " body " – not his biographical self but his created self, an effect to be apprehended as it emerges at the end of *Finnegans Wake* and is traced backwards through the stages of the changing points of view on the works which precede *Finnegans Wake*. (The " end " of *Finnegans Wake* refers not to the last page but to the halt in its production.) The point of view, for instance, produced by *Stephen Hero* and *Chamber Music* in turn produces *Dubliners ;* the point of view emerging from *Dubliners* is fixed only after Joyce arranges the stories in a chosen order – after which he said, " I cannot alter what I have written ", because that arrangement, itself, constituted the final effect. *A Portrait* is a revision of *Stephen Hero* that cannot escape the structural effect of *Dubliners,* because, as the " growth of a consciousness ", *A Portrait* is a producer not just of Stephen Dedalus as " the artist as a young man " or of Joyce's conscious aesthetics, but of a new linguistic world out of which Joyce *must* work because it cannot be willed away. The serialization of *Ulysses* contributed, perhaps, to an acceleration of the machine-like process of words working upon words in an irreversible process (Joyce called *Ulysses* a " continuation " of *Dubliners* and *A Portrait*). *Finnegans Wake* (whose serializing also effected a kind of pressure that contributes to the machine-image) is the inevitable outcome, given the total surrender to the word-machine that refuses to recognize plans and schemata intended as unifying, universalizing, completing devices. In other words, none of the works is a finished totality except by virtue of new linguistic conventions produced by resonances which then become producers of other resonances, etc., etc., so that the world of the work becomes the key to its own linguistic code. If there are " truths ", they are those engendered by the work itself, and they cannot be added up to " a truth " but are retained as disparate items ; it is these the intelligence that comes " after " apprehends as aesthetic effect (2).

Dubliners is a series of fragments based on a series of epiphanies (not the other way around) that the stories speak as " discourse " (discourse having to do with the interplay of words " spoken " as the elements are put into the art-machine). Each story therefore transcends the motivating epiphany in the process of the writing ; Joyce does not preconceive or discover the " meaning ". The

---

(2) *For some of the vocabulary used in these definitions, I have followed my own translation (and interpretation) of certain statements applicable to Joyce, as well as to Proust, in the French edition of Gilles Deleuze's Proust et les Signes* (Paris : Presses Universitaires de France, 1970).

various effects (on the author, we must remember) no doubt determine the sequential arrangement of the stories ; but only the interplay of the stories after arrangement leads to the total effect on the reader(s) and, once led to an effect, on Joyce the writer. Consider the antithesis of *Dubliners* and *Stephen Hero*. The subject matter of the early novel is the *recording* of subjective experience, whereas the short stories record (presumably) objective observations whose mysterious effect upon the subjective consciousness is left to be explored by the manner in which the language works. The process of *Dubliners* works best. Joyce lets that new point of view govern the processes of *A Portrait* ; i.e., a consciousness is the subject, but the subjective control of that consciousness is relaxed insofar as the word-machine is permitted to exert its own internal magic on the biographical material, so that a consciouness is not *remembered* and *recorded* but rather *created* as an emergent point of view. In the process, the author also " records " his aesthetics, but, by the time the product of the machine emerges, the aesthetic effect has little to do with the aesthetics mouthed by Stephen Dedalus.

Joyce begins *A Portrait* with fragments of real experience remembered. But what is *not* remembered and not recorded enters into the process in the fragments and omissions, setting up patterns which become much more important to that created consciousness than the actual experiences remembered by the creator. These emergent patterns govern election, selection, forcing a limitation upon extraneous sign-patterns determining the chapters, gradually formulating the consciousness, each of which *in*forms and so creates the stage which follows, without *con*forming to any predetermined end. The final effect is the loss of the creator's subjective self and the production of a consciousness which, by the time of its insertion into the machine of the next production, *Ulysses,* is played out, except as a component for a " discourse " among the " speaking " parts of the new novel.

Thus Stephen, in *Ulysses,* has lost Joyce's earlier voice. In fact, Stephen is freed from Joyce to the point where Bloom's voice can be listened to − another part of Joyce, perhaps, that can now be invoked. But the same thing happens in *Ulysses* that happened in *A Portrait*. Bloom may start as the personification of a desire for identification with the wily, wise, wandering and comprehensive character of Ulysses ; nevertheless, the allegorical nature of the association disappears under the dialectical processes of the word-machine − no matter how carefully the associational structure is worked out *in advance* of the production. Words, which started out to be the " active tools with which [the artist] controls, modifies, and selects the raw materials of his life " (Robert Adams), become the signs of a new life − that of the novel itself *as it draws to its close,* so that one must reread the novel from the emergent point of view in order to trace the effect.

By this time, of course, Joyce has seen that language has its own system of controls. Words as symbols have always been, for him, more important than their referents ; in fact, he has found that those referents have little to do with the power of linguistic signs. He has permitted the signs to divorce themselves from universal meanings that derive from any preconceived Logos. It is my contention that

Finnegans Wake started out to be the godlike creation of a new universe of language – one that Joyce felt he could control, through the somewhat mystical abstractions of mathematics. It was to become a Wholeness of esoteric dimensions, thereby reestablishing a Logos of language, immense in its variability and comprehensiveness, yet manipulated by a geometrical – largely circular – pattern of order. Yet the effect of *Finnegans Wake* is *not* encyclopedic assimilation and enclosure, because, in the combinations and recombinations of words upon words, words within words, sign-fragments playing against sign-fragments, repetitions vying with variations, the evocative result is disturbing precisely because it delineates even more sharply than the other works the non-linguistic void – the unspoken and unspeakable loss that the acquisition of language made certain would never be recovered. Logos is the Word all men know but can never attain in words. The effect of the production is still another point of view, insuring the repetition of endless Desire which starts the artist writing in the first place.

The Session

I

Solomon. – ...The first part of the session will be devoted to hearing from the people up here [in front of you]. I've divided them into sheep and goats. These are the sheep ; they're called the actors. And these are the goats ; they're called the reactors. I'm going to give each person a maximum of five minutes ; you may speak less than five minutes, but no longer...

[Panel members are introduced : Jacques Aubert, University of Lyons ; Roy Gottfried, Dartmouth ; Harry Staley, SUNY, Albany ; James Morrison, Princeton ; Sharon Handrock, Michael McPherson, Howard Dickler, University of Hawaii ; Mark Troy, University of Upsala.]

For this first period... there will be no participation from the audience. In the second part of the program, we shall go directly to the passage in *Finnegans Wake* that has been announced for our panel... [The audience] will have a chance for participation then.

This first [exchange], then, will be a response to the title of the session, " Joyce's Corpus as Word-Machine ". I hope that it has stirred some controversy, that it is as provocative as it should be. I'm sure that a good many people dislike thinking of Joyce's process as having anything to do with machinery. So I'm going to ask a question of the people on this side. They will respond by defining how they perceive the body of Joyce's works as a word-machine. Of course, they can respond negatively if they like. I will say, too, that none of them knows what any of the others is going to say... This is the question : Is it possible for us to define Joyce's *corpus* in these terms – as a word-machine ? How do you perceive Joyce's *corpus* as a word-machine ? What kind of a machine is it, in other words ? Or, in what way can Joyce's production be described as a machine-like process ?

Staley. − ...Edward Sapir had this to say about the nature of the relationship between thought and language ... (It sounds a little like the machine) ... " We see this complex process of the interaction of language and thought actually taking place under our eyes. The instrument makes possible the product. The product refines the instrument. The birth of a new concept is invariably foreshadowed by a more or less strained or extended use of old linguistic materials. The concept does not attain to its individual and independent life until it has found a distinctive linguistic embodiment. In most cases, the new symbol is but a thing wrought from linguistic material already in existence, in ways not [determined ?] by crushingly despotic precedents ". To be sure, it is in a struggle with language ... that Joyce developed his aesthetic strategies, and discovered and created new symbolic universes, but Joyce and Stephen, fact and fiction, were taught early on (not that they were slavish and helpless) to comprehend an entire spiritual and physical cosmos by rote − mechanically − the right words in the right order ... Joyce never forgot that fixed product of language − the Tridentine, the Council of Trent world ... whose language contributed so much to *Finnegans Wake's* search for hidden orders in art and in reality. Fixed words and word order contributed amply to Joyce's achievement in comedy. When a language goes, all goes − its world, its cosmos, its Otto Jesperson set ... One struggles against the despotic rules of language and discovers new worlds, among the components of which are to be found the vestiges of the superseded worlds. Language, the despot, is nonetheless the agent of survival, and produces the new world that shows itself after the last day : new worlds developed in the struggle against crushingly despotic grooves of language. Survival is the essential note, perhaps, of comedy. New word, new world : survival. One is tempted to say, " The comedian is the message ".

Gottfried. − I would like to take a subtly tangential tack and consider Joyce's *corpus* in a metaphorical sense, which the word itself seems to invite − that is, in organic terms. It seems to me that each work, written and rewritten over a long period of time, is an example of an internal growth. Such growth can be described in, oddly enough, Aristotelian terms which were easily available and familiar to Joyce (and to Stephen) in terms of an entelechy ... a process of actualizing possible forms, of bringing into being or into final form things which are potential and intrinsic. Remember that, in *Ulysses,* Stephen [speaks of] the self that is " preconditioned to become ". Within each work, in his entire *corpus,* there is a progression by which the work comes to a fulfillment of that which is inherent in it. The careful order, in the early stories in *Dubliners,* is a necessary prelude to the last story, " The Dead ". In the early parts of *Ulysses* − the opening chapters concerning both Stephen and Bloom − lies the potential novel that comes to realization on the progress of the long day. Practically each word of *Finnegans Wake* is the source and cause of others, reverberating throughout the book. So each text in this *corpus* grows on its own terms. As well, each text engenders the next. By defining what it is itself it makes the next possible ; it gives birth to the next. The objective distance of the narrative stance of *Dubliners* sets up the subjective process of the *Portrait.* The *Portrait's* progress, or rather progressive illumination of authorial stance, down to the sparseness of Stephen's diary entry, makes possible the combination of authorial [unintelligible word] and inner monologue of *Ulysses,* and that novel's complexity and [sounds like " prolifany ", a nice Joycean neologism !] provide − provoke rather − the variations in *Finnegans Wake.*

What I'd like to stress is that this organic process of the *corpus,* within and among parts of the *corpus,* is possible because language is organic in its own way. The Oxen of the Sun chapter in *Ulysses* is a manifesto which most clearly shows that the growth of life and the growth of language are parallel processes, synonymous processes. Language grows on its own terms and I think it's a machine in this sense − that it has rules and orders and limits just as life and all organic things have limits. It has certain patterns and rules which it fulfils as it progresses itself, as it moves. One can even say that there is an entelechy in the process of language, there's an actualization − a generation of constructions which act potentially the generative grammars. Joyce's language, machine that it might be, proliferates new possibilities, creates new forms, creates permutations of older forms. You can just see, in the entire growth, the interest in language as it moves from the interest in words (in the *Portrait)* − words with their textures, their colors − to the way language is twisted and turned in startling new ways in *Ulysses,* to the final opening up of all linguistic possibilities in *Finnegans Wake.* I think it's important to use this metaphoric sense of the word " organic " with reference to both the work and the words of Joyce, because seeing these two, I think, as organic products and methods respectively − works and words − it might be possible to posit, to suggest the created self, the body of the artist behind this whole.

Solomon. − I've heard the word " organic " used twice in opposition to the word " machine ". Maybe you [Jacques] would like to comment on that.

Aubert. − That's exactly the point I wanted to make. I haven't prepared any statements on the subject, but I react strongly against the idea of organism in regard to Joyce's work. On the contrary, the point of having a *corpus* is established on the principle that you have separate parts, and that means that things have a tendency to fall apart into pieces and into parts that are at one moment willing to work together. So this would lead us to other considerations, especially in view of psychoanalysis and what falls apart in desperation, etc. Keeping in mind the notion of organisms with reference to Joyce's work leads you to very difficult positions intellectually and metaphysically, and I would like to understand better what is the relation that you would establish between organic forms and machinery.

Morrison. − If we're going to find some sort of unification of " machine " and " organism ", perhaps we can find it in the loom. This internal contradiction between organism and machine would be most suggestively played out in the consideration of the weaving of the text. Each artist produces a text in the same way that a loom produces a textile. Each text has its own texture, which can be pulled apart, which can be put together in the consciousness of each individual reader. I like to see the machine existing outside of the text. The machine produces the text ; it's the machine as a process and not as a kind of thing within itself. Because I think within each text we see an interweaving of grammar and motif playing against one another : the diachronic aspect of the text and the synchronic aspect [interplaying]. I would like to use as [an illustration the opening of] *A Portrait,* in which we see, I think, most clearly the interweaving of grammar and motif. There's a kind of agonistic relationship; or maybe antagonistic relationship, between the simplistic grammar [along with] the fragmentation of the text, and the theme, which is the growth of both consciousness and culture at the same time. And we see in the beginning of *A Portrait* a kind of equivalence being set up between or among several kinds of beginnings. We have first of all the beginning of the story ... that story that Stephen's father is telling to Stephen about Baby Tuckoo. We also have the beginnings of consciousness in its most fragmentary form – or rather its most apparently fragmentary form – and also we see here in its beginning a kind of metaphor for the growth of culture. This interweaving is the most important aspect of the beginnings of *Portrait.* What I find most suggestive about this is the agonistic relationship between the very simplicity of the grammatical construction and the apparent fragmentation of that beginning, and the complexity of the kinds of theme and motif that are being dealt with and which are developed more fully later on. However, we can see this beginning as a kind of generative beginning for the rest of the novel. It presents all the themes, all the ideas and motifs which are developed more fully later on in the book. It's a beginning essentially about beginnings ; it's about the genesis not only of the story and of stories but also the genesis of the whole world and of culture at the same time.

Dickler. – I have a couple of reactions, one toward the use of " organic " [for the processes] of language, and I lean more towards Aubert's position. I'm not sure, as I get older, how " organic " language is, especially in writing. [I suspect] that it has nothing to do with organic growth. Especially in *Ulysses,* I get the feeling ... that what we're learning is how language exists independent of us, in a way. At best, we can control it and use it for organic reasons, but I think that one of the points of *Ulysses* is how people will read a book and then become clichés of the characters they read about and therefore become controlled by the language around them – as in advertisements. Leopold Bloom, an advertising canvasser, is a subject of the language and of the form of the " literature " of advertisement, within a very particular sort of culture. In one sense, the world is given to him and he is an object of it. Then Stephen's problem, on the other hand, is how to avoid being an object of the world and how to determine himself. He doesn't resolve this within *Ulysses.*

Now, within writing itself, the writing of any work, it seems to me that you start with certain " givens ". I think we'll find, when we get to the *[Wake]* passage later on, that there are certain things that make sense to us and are significant, having to do with myth and rhythm of life. ... A good craftsman makes these words, as blocks, relate in a way that catches this rhythm. The words don't do it themselves ; they're put together by an artist. Once you write down the first sentence of a work ... you have, say, P ; then you could have the converse of P — what is and what is not. ... The first chapter pretty much determines what the second chapter will be. In a way I suppose you can use a computer as a model. ... [At least], you get permutations of what you got from the past. The one thing I would like to remind myself is that creation of literature is a linear progression in many ways, [whereas] we want to see it organic because it's made by human beings...

McPherson. – I'd like to respond to the [idea] of machine as process and think about what that means to the reader. It seems to me that the process involves an interplay between the conscious and the unconscious, and in order for it to work the process demands that we abandon all preconceptions about what literature should be. If there is internal growth within the work, as there ought to be, there is possibility of internal growth within the reader.

Handrock. – When I think of " organism " I think of the replication of cells, each... growing larger and larger [and then repeating itself], and I don't think that's exactly what we're talking about. Also, when we use the word, " machine ", we are not talking about a production line which is popping out coke bottles all of which are exactly the same. We are talking about words, which are beginnings. As Dickler said, the first chapter determines the second chapter. But the second chapter also determines what is important in the first chapter, so the future determines the importance of the past. The resonances which are being set up are continuous in time. Until you have read the whole work you will not realize what is important, what the resonances are, until you go back. And that's why, as the author creates more works, the first work is explained by the second work, the first two works are explained by the third work, the motifs being developed continuously. Computer analogy in this sense is very good, because the resonances and the permutations are being set up in very much the same way the computer programmer sets [up his initial program] ; they change and they recreate themselves as they change.

Troy. – I think that when we talk about the word, " machine ", the printing press, the words that go into the making of the *Wake,* the mechanical process as we add each individual word to the other, we become " unquiring ones ", " un " [or Unn] being a facet of the resurrected gods. It's the name of the god, " quiring ", adding page upon page, so that [only] when we have finished reading the mechanically assembled words do we have a book. If we perceive the *Wake* at this

(3) For further elucidation of these statements, see Mark L. Troy, *Mummeries of Resurrection : The Cycle of Osiris in Finnegans Wake,* doctoral dissertation, Univertity of Uppsala, 1976 (distributor, Almquist and Wiksell International), 37 ; 45 ; 81.

level, it's no longer a composite of mechanically assembled words. It's a resurrected, living body of a god in the most literal organic sense (3). Joyce is using words that can be seen as ... placed mechanically on the page, throwing in images of sticks and stones, and whatever else. I think that we have to look at it as being organic and a soft machine in the most literal sense.

II

Solomon. – Everyone has had his initial say. I want to go directly to the passage now, and I feel that the passage itself will tell us how Joyce perceived this process. He doesn't say " machine " (and it seems that people don't like that term very well) but depicts something that moves in progression in a somewhat autonomous fashion. I am going to read the passage to you... [FW 185.27-186.8].

> Them, pious Eneas, conformant to the fulminant firman which enjoins on the tremylose terrian that, when the call comes, he shall produce nichthemerically from his unheavenly body a no uncertain quantity of obscene matter not protected by copriright in the United Stars of Ourania or bedeed and bedood and bedang and bedung to him, with this double dye, brought to blood heat, gallic acid on iron ore, through the bowels of his misery, flashly, faithly, nastily, appropriately, this Esuan Menschavik and the first till last alshemist wrote over every square inch of the only foolscap available, his own body, till by its corrosive sublimation one continuous present tense integument slowly unfolded all marryvoising moodmoulded cycle-wheeling history (thereby, he said, reflecting from his own individual person life unlivable, transaccidentated through the slow fires of consciousness into a dividual chaos, perilous, potent, common to allflesh, human only, mortal) but with each word that would not pass away the squidself which he had squirtscreened from the crystalline world waned chagreenold and doriangrayer in its dudhud.

I want to tell you why, first of all, I think that this passage tells us how Joyce perceived his *corpus*. (Of course, the way Joyce perceived it may not *be* his actual process.)

First, he thought, according to this passage, that [the *corpus*] was a sublimation of his physical body and the latter's needs. Second, he thought [the writing involved] a transformation from individuality to division, from order to chaos, and not the other way around. Third, he thought [the process was an attempt to] re-discover... the original Word, that word known to all men : all flesh, human only. Fourth, he thought that [the process] was at least semi-automatic, in that [what] happened [had to happen] as if by alchemy, a transformation of words into the Word. Fifth, he felt that the process also destroyed its input – I am using computer terms now – not only the raw materials but also the tools and machinery of the production. In other words, it ate up history, his story. In conclusion, he says [in the passage] that James Joyce was alchemically transformed by the [elusive] Word and that there would never be a finished product, only work-in-progress.

[The audience was obviously not ready to analyze the passage. One of its more vocal members was C.G. Sandelescu (University of Uppsala), who, dissatisfied by the opening comments on " word-machine ", suggested a term more appropriate than either " organism " or " machine ". (The excerpts which follow are not in strict sequential order.)]

Sandelescu. – I was glad to see that the first speaker started out with a quotation from Edward Sapir. Perhaps I'll take it up from there and say that there are dangers in analogies. The organic analogy is as dangerous as the machine analogy. I would like to refer to a whole linguistic tradition, in a sense starting from Saussure, very obvious in Sapir and later on in Whorf. I wish to suggest an alternative term... " code ". Joyce's *corpus* as " code ". The question of code creation has been insufficiently investigated in Joyce. I think we have to deal with two codes that in current linguistic research might be called " cognitive " code and " communicative " code. Let's go back to the discrepancy between language and thought. The Sapir discrepancy. He put it very bluntly and there is perhaps suggestion for discussion. What Joyce was at in *Finnegans Wake* was to achieve code fluidity, a very sophisticated kind of code fluidity, fairly close to what Troy called " soft machine " but... rather more elaborate... and what you in your conclusions called transformation from order to chaos, which is exactly the achievement of fluidity in a linguistically schlerotic code. There are striking points of similarity between the life and work of Benjamen Lee Whorf and certain points in the linguistic development and work of Joyce. Now, this question that you mentioned of the re-discovery of the Word – that would be the philosophical way of looking at it – and the transformed alchemy, and so on. What I merely want to say is that the sophisticated approach to code fluidity [makes] the relation between language and thought... in the initial quotation [Staley's reading from Sapir] emerge in a very complicated way, and this is one reason at least why Joyce's work is an open work and why *Finnegans Wake* can be interpreted the way it is interpreted.

Boyle. – I will try to say something about the process in saying something about " word-machine ". I find both these metaphors [machine and organism] valuable... But I think you need to look more, in the discussion, at the first part, the " word ". You're taking that for granted : " word-machine ", " word-organism ", and so on... I suspect that everybody in this room finds himself in the same position as I am and does not know what a word is – and is not *going* to in this life, because I figure that a word is like the flower in the crannied wall, only more a mystery. At the top of page 184 [Joyce] says, " writing the mystery of himself in furniture ". Now, I think it's most useful to realize that the word is the immediate product of the human spirit (whatever that is), and therefore the *mystery* of the word is deeply involved in the process. It comes out in the passage you've given us most vividly, when he uses out of this body the material to write on his body the word which expresses the mystery...

[The discussion, off and on, returned to the subject of the *" corpus "*.]

Staley. – In this connection... the idea of the mystery of the body... it seems the passage has something to do with Shem and possibly the Stephen-Shem progression... The body to Stephen has always, or nearly always, been repellent. We could talk perhaps about the " bowels of his misery ". He always desired to be separated from the children of Adam, sons of the flesh. He [wanted to] be made angelic, without flesh, through the alchemy of his writing. The alchemist is a kind of greedy priest, transubstantiating base metals into gold – and Joyce calls him " *alshemist* "... As he is about to turn the girl into a crane (the crane-girl in *A Portrait*), [Stephen] describes himself as a preternatural being twice, without flesh, without body, after remembering... in what dread he stood of the mystery of his own body. He would become a new, soaring, impalpable, imperishable being... out of the sluggish matter of the earth, out of the freedom and power of his soul... and this [shows] his hatred of the flesh...

Dickler. – ... The problem with Stephen, in trying to escape from his flesh, is that by doing so he's creating a world outside his words which becomes his own body ; he projects a world and then it plants itself back on top of him. When you write on the world – that is, ... when we change something in the outside world – we are making a change that is going to then change us. Now the " foolscap " or the " continuous present tense integument " is what you become surrounded with. We're surrounded by literature, surrounded by communication and information, and these become the boundaries of our knowledge. It's " cyclewheeling " ; there are certain things that... continue in cycles, but... an envelope... enshrouds us. I'm reminded that Shem is only part of a five-headed being and that HCE is... divided into parts... The " integument " is the envelope that we all live in, and we're all divided within that envelope...

Staley. – ... When [Joyce] talks about something " dividual " [in this passage], I think there is something interesting about that word. God is not " dividual " ; things that are spiritual are not " dividual ". God is simple ; *mankind* is composed of parts, therefore subject to mutability, the *corpus mutabilis*. Shem is saying that in the " transaccidentating " (not the transubstantiating), Shem has now decided, or Joyce has decided, not so much to be imperishable, simple angel, but to [be purged ?] through the fires of one's own consciousness...

[Jacques Aubert was responsible for one of the most interesting – and confusing – terms discussed : one having to do with " dividuality " and also with the impossibility of the corpus's *being perceived as an organic process.]*

Aubert. – ... We've been talking about machines, but what about the *corpus* ? It's a very simple fact that *corpus* is by definition something that is divided ; there is no *corpus* without division. For instance, we [are working on] a page today : this is a *corpus* within a *corpus*. A *corpus* does not exist without the notion of division and falling apart – something we should bear in mind in view of the coincidence in this particular text of a body falling apart, in a sense, and letters falling apart − or falling in or out at the same time. This again brings up the question of castration, which has obviously been omitted.

Troy. − ... About castration... I visualize it in terms of certain metaphors. Of course all things fall apart. You could use the same metaphor of... the body of Osiris again, falling apart into pieces which were reunited except for the phallus... an artistic creation, [made] out of wood, [by] which he recreated himself. So we start with a *corpus* that has fallen apart, but if we are going to study Joyce's *corpus* we have to re-unite it again and see the product of it.

Aubert. − We have different notions of castration... It's apparent that castration shouldn't be interpreted in terms of representation, that which can be represented, but in its relation to language, and in its relation to the production of language. That is the point I wanted to stress.

Gottfried. − It seems to me... that castration, loss, separation, etc., are in a psychological sense simply representations of death. Castration is a form of loss ; it's an ultimate loss... This brings us right back to the end of the passage. Somehow... the recreation of the artist reminds him of his own mortality. It's been brought out that Joyce's work is a process that has no end. Well, certainly it did have an end in Zurich when Joyce died. I think that in this passage the implications are that this is the " doriangrayer " of art... in a way both a transcendent life and a reminder that there is an end to the process.

Aubert. − ... Castration [is] not something *in* language ; it's something outside of language, a precondition of language... in a strict sense. There is no castration in the symbolic sense ; [in castration] there is no language at all. It is, in a sense, the organization of words, and can result in " machinery ". This type of castration is not to be discovered in language as representations of myths. it is always outside of language, a precondition of language. Have I made myself clearer ?

[The chairman tried to steer the " castration " subject toward a discussion of individuality become " dividual " through language.]

Solomon. − Something occurs in the latter part of this passage, which I think perhaps indicates Joyce's own view of his word-machine as some kind of interplay between consciousness and unconsciousness. That in itself is a division... Is it possible that in this passage Joyce suggests that what creates chaos out of order is consciousness, and can we discuss that a little bit ? Is it possible that the movement from order to chaos in the process of creativity is caused by consciousness, that it is consciousness itself that caused the division instead of the unity, the order, the oneness, etc. Somethings tells me that this passage says that Joyce's body as a body passes away when the body of his work comes into being, and that somehow this is a process from in-individuality − therefore oneness, in a way – to " dividual chaos ", and that it is through consciousness this sort of thing occurs.

Handrock. – Consciousness here, I think, refers... to language and the act of naming. In using words to put ideas down on paper, you immediately separate yourself from the oneness of all things. That is what brings the division into play, the language itself. Without language, what you have is the signified object. Once you have language, you have only signifiers ; you immediately separate yourself from the oneness of every*thing*. So it is the consciousness that is language, not the consciousness of thought and hearing, but what represents that consciousness [in discourse with] another person or creation.

Boyle. – ... That works very well with my favorite topic, the Eucharist, transaccidentated into technical terms in Catholic theology. It was made up precisely against the alchemist ; that is, transubstantiation was. Transaccidentation is brought in here... in that Joyce intends to say that he is different from Christ in his use of it [the Eucharist ?], for Christ brings his body to the accident [accidence ?] of the bread ; Joyce gives up his body to bring his soul – or his consciousness – to the body of the ink.

[Actual close analysis of the passage can be briefly reported, since there was very little ! Mark Troy called attention to the Erica tree connoted in the word, " nichthemerically ", and went on to explicate some Egyptian allusions.]

Troy. – ... If you look at " firman " in the beginning of the paragraph, " firman " is the way Frazer refers to the symbol of [the resurrected] Osiris (usually considered to be the Erica tree)... his phallus, or his... big backbone... The ejaculating wooden phallus of Osiris, here, is [Joyce's] creative pen, his " bellbearing stylo ", bearing [unintelligible] (4) (who is on the next page). The literal, physical resurrection of the god through the Erica, in " nichthemerically ", [refers to] the artist working and creating, although it's a forgery... The whole mystique of the creative god and the phallus of Osiris, Joyce's creative pen, is completely negated because it's a copy of something that never existed (5).

[The idea of " copy " was discussed somewhat differently in an exchange regarding the word " copriright " in the passage.]

McPherson. – I find it interesting that the " obscene matter " is not protected by " copriright ". " Copyright " seems to be a method of " fixing " the text, as opposed to process. The fact that it's " copriright ", rather than " copyright ", associates with copremia, which is blood poisoning due to constipation.

---

(4) Sounds like " ESET ", one of the names for Isis, or " Set ". But the context suggests " Tet ". See Troy, *Mummeries...*, 34-35.

(5) Cf; discussion of " Erica ", in Troy, *Mummeries...*, *31-32.*

Solomon. – ... We haven't discussed all the anal, fecal matter that occurs in this passage in order to relate it to creativity.

Aubert. – I was also going to say that [this lack of protection] also means that no copy can be faithful – or can be faithful protection against what is precisely at the " bottom " of the text : its preconditioning.

[So it went. This editor is now left with a feeling that something strange took place. The only way I can describe it is to say that perhaps the meeting was a destructive one in precisely the constructive way that Joyce's writing of Finnegans Wake *was destructive. Castrated, we groped madly for the " truth " that was cut from us through the language of the text. The machine of commentary grinds on. The One it seeks to create is lost to consciousness. And bodies created by the various dividing processes still believe they can assemble themselves in time. They cannot. Cutting words separate the reader from Joyce's One. " Corpus ", defined as body dead, makes sure no one can read the " truth " that came before that cutting process. But " corpus ", defined as the body of words by which a person is known to others makes sure that the castration will never be accepted.*

Margaret C. SOLOMON
University of Hawaii

Joyce's sly rhetoric *

The expanding rhetoric of Ulysses

In his essay " The Joyce Sentence ", Anthony Burgess says of *Ulysses,* " In every sentence there is a small lexical surprise – language behaving a fraction more unexpectedly " than we would find in an ordinary novelist. The surprises Burgess points out include variations on conventional word order and usage, imitative rhythms and sounds, contrasting rhythms, use of one part of speech for another, as in " warm sunshine merrying over the sea ", coinages, combinations of two or more words into one, such as " woodshadows ", almost innumerable figures of speech and a host of other devices. These unexpected usages and constructions are intended to " make it new ", in Pound's phrase, to make the reader see with fresh intensity the words or the realities they signify and imitate.

If, as Benjamin Lee Whorf and Jacques Lacan suggest, the linguistic structures in our minds dictate our perception of reality, then Joyce's purpose is to take his readers beyond conventional perceptions into alternative possibilities, actualities outside of those of which they are aware. Since these new possibilities have no system of their own, they must refer back to the established system from which they came. Thus, in every case, the reader tends to find himself suspended between the known and the unknown, the conventional and the new. Virtually every sentence, then, generates a measure of ambiguity.

I want to talk about the rhetoric of *Ulysses* in the rather sweeping terms of an overall structure which is so arranged as to lead the reader inexorably to greater and greater ambiguity and complexity. Irwin Steinberg points out that the first three episodes of *Ulysses* move from conventional narrative highlighted with

* Participants : Sheldon Brivic, Temple University ; Richard M. Kain, Louisville, Ky. ; Archie Loss, Wayne State University ; J. Mitchell Morse, Temple University, presiding.
Summaries of remarks by Messrs. Brivic, Kain and Loss ; Mr. Morse's remarks, summarized at the Symposium, have since been published in *The James Joyce Quarterly* (Winter, 1976), and are therefore not presented here.

occasional touches of stream of consciousness in " Telemachus " to pure stream in " Proteus ". As we move closer and closer to Stephen's mind, a mind preoccupied from " Nestor " with the question of possibilities which have not come into being, we become aware of a growing tangle of alternate imaginary realities which lead us into the swarming identity shifts of " Proteus ". As reality grows more complex, so does language. We move from sentences of the linguistic density of " He watched her pour into the measure and thence into the jug rich white milk, not hers " (*U* 13) to sentences like this : " Morose delectation Aquinas tunbelly calls this, *frate porcospino* " (*U* 47). The effect is like that of a mental orchestra adding instruments of association.

It might seem that as we turn from " Proteus " to " Calypso " we are going back to a simpler narrative mode. In the long run, however, " Calypso " has a more involved context than " Proteus ", primarily because Stephen has already appeared. Jean Paris reminded us yesterday that Bloom's first three episodes coincide temporally and more than temporally with Stephen's. Every detail of Bloom's world has reference to Stephen's experience as well as his own, and this becomes increasingly apparent as we move through the book and the two figures approach each other. To cite an immediate example, the love of pork kidneys because of their " fine tang of faintly scented urine " attributed to Bloom in his first paragraph (*U* 55) harks back to Stephen's feeling that mutability makes him " devour a urinous offal from all dead " (*U* 50).

Bloom appears at first to be a mere materialist and conformist, but as we move through " Calypso ", " Lotus Eaters " and " Hades ", we find that his wife is not his, that the materialism he lives in is a pipe dream, that the society that he strives to belong to excludes him. The conventional reality of Bloom and his language become at the same time unreal. Bloom's episodes also derive complexity from his positive relation to his world, as opposed to Stephen's repulsion, which allows him to perceive a greater range of material phenomena than Stephen could and puts his experience in a social context, a context of relating to others, which Stephen's expressions lack. Moreover, Bloom's episodes have organs, as Stephen's do not, and the particular organ of each episode begins to have a significant effect on the language of Bloom's thought at the cardiac incubism of " Hades ". This new level of function in the prose grows more pronounced in the windy lung prose of " Aeolus " and the speeding and slowing peristaltic esophagus prose of " Lestrygonians ". The well-known rhetorical richness of " Aeolus " impresses upon the reader an augmented awareness of what language is doing figuratively which should stay with him at least to book's end. " Lestrygonians " sets up a complicated series of correspondences between different foods and mental states and between the alimentary process and the life cycle as well as setting up a deep opposition between Bloom's past and his present − connections that reverberate and exfoliate later.

" Scylla and Charybdis " builds a vast labyrinth of Shakespearean and Homeric parallels which intertwines Stephen and Bloom and lends increased density of reference to subsequent material. " Wandering Rocks " contains nineteen sections, all of which refer to all of the other eighteen and to all of the episodes in the book. This central episode provides new conceptions of reflexiveness and of time and space as frames for experience. The use of music in " Sirens " gives us a prose consistently further from practical, denotative language than anything which has yet appeared. From here our increased awareness of language as an abstract construction as well as medium of presentation will generally continue to provide another aspect of what we read.

" Cyclops " provides the greatest variety and range of world views and linguistic structures yet incorporated in the book. Its contrasting juxtaposition of various inflated value systems in language forces the reader to review the values of his world of words. " Nausikaa " only presents two basic levels of reality, but each of these levels has more weight and depth than anything in " Cyclops ". In showing Gerty MacDowell and Bloom's attitude toward her, Joyce plunges his dividing scalpel deeper into the corpus of conventional thought by an original and disturbing analysis of some of the most sacred and transcendent areas of feeling.

By " Oxen of the Sun ", any sentence is capable of referring not only to the main characters and their various levels of perception and symbolism, but also to a writer, usually from the past, and to his era of English cultural history as well as to a phase of foetal development and its physiological characteristics.

" Circe " carries the recapitulation of previous chapters to new lengths and distorts ordinary reality with unprecedented vigor to make us aware of submerged possibilities in the mind : the major new level added in this episode is deeply unconscious. " Eumaeus " may seem dull – in fact it is dull, and it may be an exception to the book's pattern of mounting polyphony; but its contrasts between cliché and insight give new development to the function of language as obstacle, which is prominent in the *Nostos,* once the reader has learned in " Circe " what language hides. Moreover, Stephen and Bloom commune with each other for the first time in " Eumaeus ", and the actual relationship of Stephen and Bloom, though it has been building all along is a new entity, a new dimension of possibilities which were not present in the two individuals.

" Ithaca " ranges further in time and space than any other episode and draws in new areas of reference and documentation in such directions as science and history. But the central innovation of " Ithaca ", and one of the major innovations of *Ulysses,* lies in the questions " Ithaca " raises about the ultimate values of almost all of Joyce's readers : logic and reason themselves, which are isolated against a background of interstellar space so that they are manifested as somnambulistic ritual.

Having gotten this far, where are we going ? The structure of *Ulysses* orders the whole and influences each part toward a steady multiplication of levels of meaning and possibility. As the book gains dimensions, it gets closer to reality, for reality includes infinite possibilities and any system or language can only cover a small part of these. But as the book gets more multivalent, polysemous and complex, it grows more and more uncertain. Ellmann, in *Ulysses on the Liffey,* reminds us that Joyce's universe is built on uncertainty. Joyce agreed with Lawrence that when we deal with certainties, we deal with dead things, and that only in the realm of uncertainty can we find possibilities for life. Richard Rowan of *Exiles* insists that his burden of doubt gives his beloved Bertha life, at least in his mind. Joyce believed that we live in the minds of those who love us. The agony of uncertainty through which Bloom meanders daydreaming in *Ulysses* is what makes possible the tremendous vitality Molly shows in the last episode, which Joyce called the " countersign to Bloom's passport to eternity ".

Ulysses builds up the possibility of relation between Stephen, Bloom and Molly suggested by its many mythological references, supernatural signs and coincidences. On the realistic level, the three fail to communicate and drift by each other, but the possibility of their union remains present as an ideal and perhaps as an invisible spiritual process in the background. Thus, *Ulysses* is both affirmative and ironic, both comic and tragic. The entire book is constructed so as to lead progressively to a maximum final revelation of uncertainty, and the stasis with which it ends is held in place by balanced opposing forces pushing outward in all directions.

Sheldon BRIVIC
Temple University

The Magic of Joyce's Style

In thinking of Joyce's stylistic virtuosity I am reminded of the statement attributed by Suetonius to Augustus Caesar : " He so improved the city that he justly boasted he had found it brick and left it marble ". It would require a seminar to demonstrate this fully in *Ulysses,* much more time, a life in fact, to follow it through the Joyce canon. A dissertation by Eberhard Kreutzer, *Sprache und Spiel im 'Ulysses' von James Joyce* (Bonn : Bouvier, 1969),analyzes with Teutonic thoroughness Joyce's *lautmalerei, gestaltsymbolik, klangmagie, wortwitz, namenfunktion,* and other rhetoric devices, with an index of more than 150 pages, listing instances of sound painting, form symbolism, sound magic and wit from the " Able " of the old palindrome to the " zrads " of the rocket display in " Nausicaa ".

I present but one illustration here, but before doing so I shall mention two major factors that entered into Joyce's " sound magic ". A love of music, coupled with a pleasant tenor voice, and a prodigious memory for songs is the first aspect. The second is his constant preoccupation with words. Both have been extensively documented by critics, biographers, and compilers of concordances.

Now for my illustration. William M. Schutte's fine book, *Joyce and Shakespeare* (1957), contains a most interesting appendix that lists the passages from three leading Shakespeare biographers, sources Joyce adapted in Stephen's theory, as expounded in the library scene of *Ulysses.* From the then popular biographies by Georg Brandes, Sidney Lee, and Frank Harris, Joyce derived most of his biographical data. In fact, Dedalus even adopts from Brandes the device of dramatizing a typical afternoon performance at the Globe Theatre. Chapter VIII of the Second Book of Brandes' biography begins with an imagined performance of " Julius Caesar " :

> It is afternoon, a little before three o'clock. Whole fleets of wherries are crossing the Thames... full of theatre-goers who have delayed a little too long over their dinner and are afraid of being too late; for the flag waving over the Globe Theatre announces that there is a play to-day.

Brandes goes on to describe playbills on the streets, the filling of the theater, the three trumpet blasts and the parting of the curtain.

Here and elsewhere Brandes is, even in translation, not a bad narrator; it is straightforward stuff. But see what Joyce does, with the time of day and the flag waving on its mast :

> – It is this hour of a day in mid June, Stephen said, begging with a swift glance their hearing. The flag is up on the playhouse by the bankside.

" It is this hour ", that is, a bit before three o'clock, " of a day in mid June ". *Ulysses,* we all remember, takes place on a day in mid June. Notice too, the immediacy of Stephen's presentation : " begging with a swift glance their hearing ". " The flag is up " – again a direct descriptive statement, with no explanation.

Mr. Schutte cites 64 details that Joyce took from the three commentators, and transcribes the original statements. In every case Joyce has made them marble by means of rhythm, alliteration, or vivid phraseology. One more example must suffice. Brandes describes the bustling activity on the ground level : " Refreshment-sellers moved about among them, supplying them with sausages and ale, with apples and nuts ". Again, a fair enough description. Here is Joyce : " Canvasclimbers who sailed with Drake chew their sausages among the groundlings ". That is word magic.

Richard M. KAIN
Louisville, Kentucky

Painting and Ulysses

How useful is an interarts approach to an examination of Joyce's rhetoric in *Ulysses* or, more generally, to an examination of his style ?

It is obvious that in certain respects Joyce sought to create such connections in *Ulysses* (" Sirens " and music, " Nausikaä " and painting), but it is also obvious that, as the central work of fiction in the modernist movement, *Ulysses* creates its own connections with such movements as Cubism, Futurism, and even Surrealism – connections which might more properly be called, in Ralph Cohen's term, " intersections ".

Indeed, the interarts approach to the study of Joyce's rhetoric or style is most useful when it seeks out such analogies. The closest connection between *Ulysses* and Cubism, for example, lies in their common syntax : the rhetoric of fragmentation. The example of Bloom's impression of Boylan (*U* 83 : 12) is familiar : it is analogous to the Cubist technique, pervasive in *Ulysses,* of letting the part represent the whole. The headlines or captions in " Aeolus " – though perhaps providing an instance of the direct influence of collage – represent yet another instance of the same sort of analogy, in " Aeolus " summed up by the art of the chapter. Aesthetically, such techniques – despite the differences between the media involved – have similar effects. Epistemologically, their relationship can be stated this way : the movement of Joyce's narrative beyond causation has as its counterpart in Cubist painting the movement beyond illusionism and perspective. As prose fiction, through Joyce, moves toward simultaneity in narrative – a temporal flattening in which past, present, and future exist on the same plane – so painting, through Cubism, moves toward a fragmenting, and flattening, of the object – a reduction of the picture surface to two dimensions and a rearrangement of the subject at the will of the artist on the picture plane. Both Joyce's narrative and Cubist painting abandon traditional modes of realism to achieve, at least in part, a new kind of realism – in one case through a greater specificity and truth of detail, in the other through a greater inventiveness and flexibility of materials and forms.

This specificity in Joyce's work constitutes a form of rhetoric in itself, and, one way or another, always figures in discussion of how Joyce's work achieves symbolic meaning : there is frequently a tension between the person, object, or event described in Joyce's work and the larger meaning that the description is supposed to imply. The dinner table described in detail in " The Dead " overflows with abundance and life, the very qualities the characters of the story largely lack. The vital language of the description reinforces this lack, as it does in many places in similar contexts in *A Portrait* and *Ulysses.*

This feature of Joyce's work – I think sometimes his most notable achievement, till I think of the several dozen others – compares strikingly with the techniques of a number of contemporary representational artists – most notably, to my view Jasper Johns. In Johns' early work the thing represented and the technique of representation have nearly equal aesthetic value. (Most students of the aesthetics of painting would argue that it is not possible to make such a distinction even for purposes of discussion; however, for purposes of discussion, I must make it). We are struck both by the object, which is plain (a Ballantine ale can; a can of Savarin coffee) and by the absolutely impeccable technique by which it is rendered. Our " understanding " of the painting depends upon our grasping the essential irony of such impeccable technique applied to such perishable, even flimsy, subject matter. The work lives by means of such rendering, thereby achieving uniqueness and integrity. (Shades of Stephen, both in *Portrait* V and at the beginning of " Proteus " !)

Painting of course does not provide the only area in which useful and illuminating interarts study can take place in connection with Joyce's work, but, because of its important place in the history of modernism, and because of the importance to the study of literature of the pictorial tradition in general, it provides perhaps the best examples. The ultimate value of the interarts approach lies in its serving to identify larger stylistic trends and their relationship to cultural values, with all the ambiguity and difficulty that such study involves. In Joyce's case I believe that such study leads us to see that his ultimate achievement as an artist is to be measured in terms of realism and the realistic tradition – in terms, that is, of his early proximity to realism and his gradually increasing distance from it.

Archie LOSS
Wayne State University

Political perspectives
on Joyce's work *

Beja. – I'd like to welcome you to the panel on political perspectives on Joyce's work. Yesterday's talk by Richard Ellmann gave us a sort of context; but otherwise, the topic we have come together to discuss today is not one that's been treated very often at Joyce Symposia : as a matter of fact, not even, with some exceptions, very frequently in Joyce criticism. Indeed, we sense in reading many critics who are interested in the political implications of literature that they regard us, Joyceans, if not necessarily always Joyce himself, as of the other camp. In his later years to be sure Joyce himself, at least at times, seemed to encourage that sort of approach or, if you will, lack of approach. For a few years in his early manhood, he often liked to refer to himself as a Socialist, but as time went on he more frequently expressed complete cynicism in regard to all political ideas – though as always with Joyce, it's not easy to tell how much irony or seriousness or Joycean blend of irony and seriousness there may be in his remarks. The most notorious of them was one he reportedly made to Stanislaus Joyce in 1936 : « For God's sake don't talk about politics. I'm not interested in politics. The only thing that interests me is style. »

Well, the people we've brought together today for this panel are themselves not uninterested in style, nor are they uninterested in politics, yet they're all very, very interested in James Joyce. They are :

Bernard Benstock, who teaches at the University of Illinois at Champaign-Urbana and who is of course one of the most prominent Joyceans around; in addition to being the author of such books as *Joyce-Again's Wake,* he is one of the founders of the Joyce Foundation and of the nice idea of having these Symposia.

« Moderator » Morris Beja

Members of Panel : Bernard Benstock, Seamus Deane, Paul Delany, Leslie Fiedler, Suzette A. Henke, Maria Jolas, Philippe Sollers.

Note : Readers will occasionally notice various discrepancies between the original French of Philippe Sollers and the English version; the translation was kindly made on the spur of the moment under difficult conditions, and it could not be expected to be either complete or perfect. However, we have made only a few changes and additions, in order to preserve the atmosphere of the discussions as they actually took place.

Leslie Fiedler is Samuel L. Clemens Professor of English – a wonderful title to have – at the State University of New York at Buffalo, where he is also Chairman, presumably a not so wonderful title to have. A novelist as well as a critic he, as everybody here will know, is the author of some of the most influential critical studies of the last couple of decades.

Seamus Deane is Statutory Lecturer in the Department of English at University College, Dublin. As one whose own background is Northern Ireland, he has himself spoken out on the controversies of his time and place. As a critic, he has written illuminatingly about French as well as Irish literature, and as a poet he has produced a fine volume of poems called *Gradual Wars.*

Paul Delany teaches at Simon Fraser University in Canada; he is the author of *British Autobiography in the Seventeenth Century,* but as evidence of his breadth of interest he has been awarded a Guggenheim Fellowship for next year to aid him in his study of the reaction of D. H. Lawrence to World War One.

Suzette Henke teaches at the University of Virginia in the English Department, and she has published critical studies in the *James Joyce Quarterly* and elsewhere, and has a forthcoming article – dealing, incidentally, with sexual politics – in *American Imago.* She is at work on a book-length phenomenological study of *Ulysses* entitled *Joyce's Moraculous Sindbook.*

To introduce Maria Jolas to any group of Joyceans would be superfluous, and to do so in Paris would border on the ridiculous.

Philippe Sollers is another unnecessary introduction in Paris. He is of course a prominent critic and novelist and the editor of *Tel Quel,* one of today's most influential literary journals. Next to him is Elizabeth Chardanel (?) who has agreed to translate for us and for M. Sollers. M. Sollers has asked to start off our discussion.

Sollers. – Le sujet de cette réunion ce sont les perspectives politiques de l'œuvre de James Joyce. Et je voudrais tout de suite pour expliquer ma présence dire quel effet politique me paraît avoir aujourd'hui le symposium international qui se tient à Paris cette année.

Par effet politique, je ne veux pas dire que je veux parler politique. Je vais parler des effets politiques qui sont produits par la tenue de ce symposium. Je vais faire deux réflexions – une sérieuse, et une autre plaisante. Normalement, étant donné que le symposium s'ouvrait non pas ici mais dans le grand amphithéâtre de la Sorbonne, qui a été occupé par les étudiants en mai '68, normalement ce symposium devait être présidé par le Recteur de la Sorbonne. Or, on a vu apparaître, visiblement très gêné, un fonctionnaire de l'Éducation Nationale pour expliquer que ni le Secrétaire d'État, ni le Recteur ne pouvait assister à l'inauguration de ce symposium sur Joyce. Et ceci s'est passé devant l'Ambassadeur d'Irlande et un représentant de l'Ambassade d'Angleterre. Vous voyez que nous sommes tout de suite dans la politique. Et je tiens à dire que comme intellectuel français, je veux excuser la grossièreté de l'État français dans cette affaire. Et je pense que c'est bien que ce soit moi qui m'excuse en son nom, puisque je le combats politiquement.

S'il y avait eu, je suis sûr, un colloque sur Proust en Nouvelle Zélande, je suppose que les autorités locales auraient été présentes. Ma seconde observation, très rapidement, c'est que cette inauguration que l'État n'a pas voulu accomplir (parce qu'on peut toujours se libérer pour être présent à un événement de cette importance), cette inauguration a été confié à la parole d'un psychanalyste prestigieux. L'État se retire mais la psychanalyse reste. On aurait pu imaginer, mais c'est probablement là qu'est l'affaire politique... On aurait pu demander à un écrivain français, à supposer qu'il en existe encore, ce qui n'est pas sûr, d'ouvrir sur un écrivain – un colloque sur Joyce. La question politique que je pose : Est-ce que le gouvernement et la psychanalyse savent s'il y a oui ou non, aujourd'hui, un écrivain français en France ? Voilà, c'était pour expliquer ma présence.

Translator. – The subject of this meeting is the political perspectives on James Joyce's work. Philippe Sollers, to explain why he is here today, would like to explain the political impact in fact of the Symposium which is taking place in Paris this week.

When he says political effect, he doesn't say he's going to talk politics, but discuss the specific political impact of this Symposium here in Paris – which is not precisely the same thing. First, a serious remark, then a joke. The opening of the Symposium was not to be here but at the Sorbonne, the place which was occupied by students in May 1968, so the Rector of the Sorbonne should have attended the first meeting. He wasn't here. A civil servant came who looked rather embarrassed and said in a rather embarrassed way that neither the Rector nor the Minister, the State Secretary, could attend the meeting. This was in the presence of the Irish ambassador and someone representing the British ambassador. You see that we are immediately in the world of politics. Being a French intellectual, he would like to excuse the French government for being so rude in this. It is well that he should make excuses because he is himself personally fighting the French government.

He says if there had been a Symposium on Proust in New Zealand, local authorities would have been there. So this opening that the government did not want to attend (it is always possible to free oneself in order to be present at such a significant event), this opening was entrusted to a very famous psychoanalyst. The state exits while psychoanalysis remains. One could imagine that one could have asked a French writer, if there is still such a thing as a French writer today, to open a Symposium concerning a writer; this would have been a possibility. So he is going to ask a question : do the French government and the psychoanalysts know if there is still such a thing as a French writer in France today ? This is why he wanted to explain why he is here today.

Beja. – And I think he's done us the good service of reminding us, in case we were in danger of forgetting, to recognize the political perspectives relevant not just to Joyce but to us as Joyceans if you will.

The rest of the panel, I should explain, will not be making any sorts of formal presentations, or reading any papers and so on. After a while, I hope we can open things to the audience. Perhaps the way that we can start is for me to ask if any other people on the panel have anything in particular they'd like to bring out, any particular question that they believe ought to be raised, or a particular perspective that ought to be taken.

Jolas. – I'd just like to make a comment. Joyce always said that there was nothing simple in anything that concerned James Joyce.

Beja. – You said that very simply.

Jolas. – That's all I wanted to say.

Beja. – I'd like to throw out a question. And that is, how do we react to that earlier quotation ? How, in the light of the points for example that M. Sollers has made, do we react to Joyce's remark that he's not interested in politics – that the only thing that interests him is style ? First of all, there is the question of how serious he may have been. Let's assume he was serious. Is the remark relevant to us ? Does it relate in any important way to his work ? Anybody want to respond to that ?

Henke. – I want to respond by saying, isn't this what we as academics are accused of all the time : of not being interested in politics, of being interested only in style ? And I'm sure that most of you have fought this battle on your particular campus or at your university many times : the battle, the question, is art relevant ? Is twentieth-century literature relevant to the students who are studying today ? Well I think it is relevant for a number of reasons. But I now want to respond to what Murray was saying : how do we react to Joyce saying he's not interested in politics ?

I think that Joyce means he's not interested in politics as it is understood in terms of political science. But when Joyce was asked why he was a pacifist, why he so hated and eschewed violence, he answered that he felt the violence of birth and death was traumatic enough for him. He didn't need inter-personal conflict in addition to that. I see Joyce's work as highly political but within a much larger context. I think in all of his work, he recognizes men and women as political beings; but he also has a keen sense of the existential violence at the heart of existence : the violence of birth and death which must not be exacerbated by war, conflict, hatred, etc. And I myself, as a pacifist, keep trying to explain to people that pacifism is not an apolitical stance. It is highly political, but it is not political in the usual sense of the word. I'm always surprised to find people reading *Ulysses* and saying, well, what political relevance does that have ? – Joyce makes one allusion to the Russo-Japanese War. But I think that the whole of *Ulysses* shows a tremendous compassion for human beings as political animals, as political people. Joyce shows remarkable understanding of economic limitations, almost in a

Marxist sense – economic limitations that somehow constrain personal creativity and personal art. And he has enormous compassion for people who are alienated from themselves, alienated from their work, and who are in some way enslaved, almost literally, to the exigencies of bed, board, and breeding.

We see this throughout *Ulysses* in terms of Leopold Bloom's monologue and the thoughts that go through his mind. Very early in the narrative, when he goes to the Burton pub and he sees people eating, masticating gristle, devouring various foods, he's horrified. Not so much by the grotesque glee of all these people munching away, but by the realization that there is a kind of Darwinian substratum to existence, that there's an ethic of survival that leads us all to fight for existence. He's horrified to realize that the ethic by which we are motivated is an instinct to kill or be killed, eat or be eaten. So in the course of *Ulysses,* Bloom has got to get beyond the Darwinian ethic of survival to a recognition of *caritas* – to a recognition of the possibility of human love in terms of *agape,* as opposed to the Darwinian aggressive militant ethic, the ethic of fools.

I would like to suggest that Joyce's pacifism really does pervade everything he writes, because later on in " Cyclops " when Bloom says, I'm not talking about hatred, I'm talking about the opposite of hatred, love, he's talking not only about political pacifism – the fact that British force is the same as Irish force – he's also talking about his own domestic situation. Because much earlier, when he was horrified by people eating each other, cannibalizing one another, he was also horrified by his own identification with MacTrigger in the stewpot, feeling very much as if Boylan were cannibalizing on him. Boylan is fitter sexually to survive. He's more potent. And so Bloom, in turning away from an ethic of force, is also turning away from the possibility of literally enforcing Molly's fidelity by following Boylan, or chaperoning her rehearsal with Boylan, or trying to catch Boylan and Molly in the act. He's almost justifying his seemingly impotent behavior and silence later on in " Cyclops " when he says, I'm talking about love – the opposite of hatred, the opposite of force. He realizes that Molly is not a possession, not a piece of property, and that he can't lose what he never possessed.

Benstock. – You know it's very difficult in a controversy to respond to so much opinion and information, and I don't want to use the dishonest opening that says, I agree with everything that Professor Henke has said, *but...*

Beja. – Get to the but, get to the but.

Benstock. – Let's go back to the first few points that you make, because thereafter I was in such harmonious disagreement that I was practically stultified at the degree...

Henke. – Harmonious disagreement !

Benstock. – Harmonious disagreement. The first part of that opening salvo : there is a very serious danger to me of over-identification. Because Joyce is a pacifist and I am a pacifist, Joyce and I are equal as -pacifists. Because I am a Marxist, I would like Joyce to be a Marxist.

Beja. – Does that mean if I write, I write like Joyce ?

Benstock. – If only that worked out as harmoniously for me as it does for Professor Henke – actually it doesn't. But more important, back to the initial question : when Joyce set up a conflict between politics on one end and style on the other, look at how many steps were jumped in the interim. I think perhaps we may have to fill in some of those steps. How did we get a dichotomy between politics and style ? In between somewhere is obviously literature. In the absence of an answer, I would like to rephrase that question for that center. What is the relationship in that joco-serious comment about politics and style that actually sets up the tension between them ?

Deane. – I guess as Irish, I want to point to one thing that I think is important in relation to Joyce's politics, and that is the fact that like most if not all Irish writers, Joyce is a colonial writer. And colonialism I think could be identified in his work by two features. One is the feature of frozen time, the degree to which he freezes – not the actual political Ireland that was in a state of severe disarray in fact – during the time that he wrote and which he ignored. But he pulls it emblematically into a kind of a post-Parnell tradition of defeat, of the lost leader, given up to the mob. There's a colonial aspect to this, and I think one could find affiliations with the literature of the southern United States, the literature of Mexico, the literature of any particular area which has suffered severe economic, military and political defeat.

I think what Joyce is trying to do in his work, as Yeats sought in a different way in his work, is to try and take the country as an emblem – emblem of defeat, emblem of law – and to transfigure and transmute that frozen country into a tradition of artistic triumph and integrity. And I think if one looks at the evolution of his work, with *Ulysses* certainly as central work all right, but a work that I think in a big way, in a kind of ersatz way, attempts to reproduce via the Molly Bloom soliloquy a sense of human solidarity – which in fact I don't think that the total novel can bear. Because what Joyce finally does, the very appropriate thing – exactly the same thing that Yeats was doing for a good deal of his life anyway – in *Finnegans Wake,* isn't it, is to take history, Irish history, as the central nucleus around which European and world history is built, and to try and transmute history into art. And in transmuting history into art, he is transmuting in fact Irish politics into style. But it's a politics of defeat, it's a style of triumph. And it's the relationship between those two, I think, that's part of the tension which governs the work of Joyce, governs the work of Beckett, to a great degree governs the work of Yeats, and certain other Irish writers – but particularly those three. And I think this is a classic colonial cast of mind. It's a cast of mind in which in a way what the colonial writer is attempting to do is to take the cosmopolitan form that he has inherited from the colonizing country, the form of the novel, and to repossess that form, to if you like reconquer the territory of the conqueror, but via style : there is no other means by which it can be done.

And of course when we say this, when we say that there is no other means by which it can be done, we realize the degree to which Joyce was disassociated from the revolutionary politics of the turn of the century in Ireland − even more so than was Yeats. And, I think, that kind of dissociation in the literary sphere has been a typical feature of Irish life since Parnell and in fact I suppose even more strongly since the Famine, that shock that still has its repercussions in the Irish mentality. And Joyce is one of the greatest exemplars of this translation of history into writing and into style.

Beja. − I might mention in relation to this an accusation, and I wonder if you could react to it, that Conor Cruise O'Brien once made, that Joyce acted like that English minister of the − well I forgot exactly when − but I think the 1920's, who remarked at one time, I was never present while a revolution was going on. Do you think that that's a fair accusation against Joyce in terms of Irish history ?

Deane. − Yes, that's a fair accusation, and yet it's unfair because of course Joyce thought that where he was was where the revolution was taking place. And in a way it was true. But there were two revolutions. There was the revolution, the anti-colonial revolution that exploded in 1916, about which he knew practically nothing. He knew a good deal about the spirit that governed that revolution, but I think on the other hand Joyce would have been one of those who would have agreed with the remark that revolutions are never sophisticated. They are great necessary simplifications, and for an Alexandrian artist, a baroque, rococo mind like that, he couldn't have a revolution that didn't take a complicated form. But in Ireland it took the brutal, simplistic form of analysis, action, and then collapse. With that he has nothing to do.

Beja. − [After a note was slipped to the moderator :] The note that was passed up to me says, " Ah ça IRA ", which I think roughly translated would be Up the IRA. [In response to a question about the writer of the note :] A nameless person − McIntosh.

Sollers. − [Placing a book on the table :] Je vous montre une révolution.

Translator. − He shows you one revolution.

Beja. − That is a copy of *Finnegans Wake.*

James Atherton, in audience. − I wonder if you would react to the notion that in *Finnegans Wake* Joyce is defeating the English by taking English from them.

Beja. – Well it is possible to respond to that by saying that one wonders if he chose to refuse to write in the language of the conqueror in his last work, but he did not, as other Irish writers have decided to do, write in Irish – perhaps because he would rather not use the language of the conquered – and between those two he chose *Finnegans Wake*. But I would not be comfortable defending that very long.

Fiedler. – Surely one of the most political aspects of Joyce is his choice of language. There is the implicit politics of the language in which one chooses to write if one has a choice, or if at least his friends are telling him that he has a choice of language. And the interesting thing about *Ulysses* – which of all Joyce's books I know best, and which I always end up talking about whenever I pretend to talk about Joyce – is that in *Ulysses* there are three languages everywhere. One is English, the language of the imperial conquerors, and the other two languages, which are everywhere, are the languages of the Roman Church – that is to say Latin in the first place and Italian in the second place. All that Joyce presumably said he was fighting against in what comes close to a political statement – the mastership of Ireland by English imperialism on the one hand, and the dictatorship of the Church on the other hand – he gives way to by using those two languages, and the book *Ulysses* itself is an attack on the use of Irish. It's not simply that he doesn't use Irish. The best speaker of Irish in that book is a dog, Garryowen, right ? – and that, like many of Joyce's jokes, is a joke which is very much to the point.

And in a way Joyce is in a position very much like the position of Kafka writing in German rather than in Czech. There is an implicit politics and there is a bad conscience always in that. I don't pretend to be an authority on Irish literature, but I have heard people who know much more about this say over and over again that any Irish writer who writes in English suffers to some degree from a bad conscience. And what Joyce finally did in *Finnegans Wake* was to attempt to turn English into his own language. But he didn't win that fight because the book is written in a language which is based on English. The language of *Finnegans Wake* is English as much as the language of Milton's *Paradise Lost* is English. They are both languages based on English and distorted by a person of talent. But it's still English and outside of English he never got. That's one of the two things, two aspects of politics. But one other comment. The statement that I'm not interested in politics, I'm interested in style, is a political statement. Precisely.

Beja. – That's true. An essay by Paul Delany ends with that remark if I remember correctly, and it is a Marxist critique of Joyce, concentrating on *Dubliners*. And I wonder if we might confront, since we've already gotten to *Finnegans Wake,* an implication I believe is in that essay : that Joyce's career, from a political perspective, declines after the early work. Or is that unjust as a summary ?

Delany. – Well I think, as everybody here will know, that there's a very obvious... flirtation I think is the best word with Socialism by Joyce in his early years, or through the period of about 1904 to 1907. Now I'm saying that for a relatively short period in his youth up to about 1907 Joyce clearly did flirt with Socialism, but that for I think essentially personal reasons in 1907 with the composition of " The Dead " and the undertaking of the *Portrait* he decided that that was a horse that was not going to run as far as he was concerned. And I think from that point onwards what we see in Joyce is an elaborate rationalization of the possibility of the existence of progressive political development in Ireland. So that when somebody like Sheehy-Skeffington was murdered in 1916, Joyce's reaction as far as we can tell was very frigid, because he had discounted in advance the possibility of there being a revolution in Ireland. That's almost a kind of magic thinking I think on Joyce's part, like when somebody discussed with Lawrence the possibility of a second world war he said, there can't be one, I won't have it. And Joyce's remark that Ireland will die for me is in the same vein.

There are these personal necessities which made it impossible for him to enter into progressive political development after 1907. The whole obsession with the idea of betrayal as the peculiarly Irish style of politics entered into that. So I think what one can say for Joyce after that period is that he has very important negative virtues among the great English writers of our century, who I assume are Eliot, Pound, Lawrence, and Yeats, and he was the only person in that group of five who was not contemptuous of ordinary people, of their interests, their aspirations, their sexuality, anything about them. And as Gide said, after the revolution Joyce should be left alone. But I think in political terms, it was only those negative virtues that survived : let's say the pacifism, the mistrust of authority, the dislike of the anti-semitism and flirtation with or commitment to Fascism of people like Wyndham Lewis and Pound; but beyond that I think temperamentally he was not inclined to go.

Sollers. – Je voudrais qu'on essaie de revenir à l'effet politique de l'écriture de Joyce, et surtout à l'effet politique de l'écriture de *Finnegans Wake*. Je me demande simplement si les gens qui parlent anglais ici, et nous parlons pour la plupart anglais. Vous êtes en majorité anglais et moi je parle français, ce qui fait que je me sens un peu opprimé en minorité. Je me demande simplement si vous avez conscience que depuis que ce livre a été écrit, l'anglais n'existe plus. Et pourtant, tout le monde va continuer pendant très longtemps à parler une langue morte, de même que l'église catholique a continué à parler latin. Par conséquent, nous avons un problème politique très important : c'est ce petit espace de langues vivantes et un énorme espace de langues mortes. Je compare cette situation à celle de Dante au XIVᵉ siècle. On sait que Joyce et d'autres écrivains de l'époque se sont intéressés très profondément à Dante. Et je crois que pour comprendre la profondeur de la tentative de Joyce, nous devons prendre cette référence très loin dans le temps. Comme, par exemple, Engels l'avait très bien vu en disant que le fait de passer du latin à l'italien était une révolution considérable parce que, justement, le capitalisme allait venir. Dante représente la première très grande révolution qui n'est pas seulement économique mais qui consiste à changer de langues. Et peut-être que lorsque Joyce ne voulait pas qu'on lui parle de politique, c'est qu'il voyait que la façon que les gens avaient de parler politique coupait complètement ce problème de la révolution économique, de la révolution dans la langue. Et c'est pour ça qu'il insistait sur son travail, puisqu'il est même allé jusqu'à dire qu'on ferait mieux de s'occuper de *Finnegans Wake* que de l'invasion de la Tchécoslovaquie. La vraie question en profondeur : c'est pourquoi la politique se parle-t-elle en langues mortes ? Parce que les enjeux politiques de Joyce ont été très importants dans le Marxisme, par exemple, dans les discussions entre Lukács et Brecht. Mais c'est toujours le dogmatisme de la langue morte qui semble l'emporter.

[Interruption]

Sollers. – Alors, je peux continuer ?

Beja. – Certainly.

Sollers. – J'essaie seulement de dire ce que Joyce me semble avoir essayé de faire : déclarer la guerre à une langue nationale. Il le dit lui-même : « J'ai déclaré la guerre et j'irai jusqu'au bout ». Ça veut dire qu'en s'appuyant sur une langue qui a été effacée de l'histoire, le gaélique, voulant détruire une langue imposée, l'anglais, pour aller vers toutes les langues, pourquoi a-t-il voulu faire sa révolution en utilisant le maximum de langues ? Justement pour marquer que la fin des nationalités était décidée. Et ça, c'est un acte d'une portée politique immense.

D'autre part, voulant toucher l'inconscient. Or, précisément l'attachement à une langue nationale c'est, nous le savons par la psychanalyse, les investissements préconscients. C'est pourquoi la majorité des gens qui sont enfermés dans une langue refuse à la fois l'inconscient et le débat international. Joyce veut détruire le nationalisme, mais il va plus loin que l'internationalisme. Ce qu'il est en train de construire avec ce livre, c'est un trans-nationalisme. Car le langage de l'internationalisme est aussi gagné par la mort, est parlé aussi dans une langue morte.

Donc, quel est son acte politique au fond ? Il va désarticuler, analyser, réarticuler et, en même temps, annuler le maximum de traces, de résidus culturels, idéologiques, historiques, mythologiques, linguistiques et religieux. Son obstination à analyser la religion est ici son geste politique le plus important. Car si nous prenons la religion comme le phénomène fondamentalement névrotique de l'humanité, on est obligé de constater que, à part Joyce, personne ne semble avoir réussi à sortir de l'espace religieux. Et pourquoi lui, sinon parce qu'il a obtenu à travers son écriture, un certain savoir sexuel fondamental sur l'espèce. Donc pour moi Joyce c'est la même ambition que Freud : analyser 2 000 ans d'humanité et pas se concentrer sur dix ans de politique. C'est pour ça que l'acte de Freud est aussi très long (?). Et le fascisme l'a toujours compris. Les premiers livres qu'on interdit sont ceux de Freud. Et je dirai que *Finnegans Wake* est le livre le plus formidablement anti-fasciste que l'on a écrit dans l'entre-deux-guerres, alors que le fascisme gagne toute l'Europe. La production d'un dirigeant fasciste est ruinée profondément par cette écriture, parce qu'elle ruine toutes les idéologies. C'est l'acte le plus fort, en effet, contre la paranoia politique. C'est pourquoi il est très drôle mais aussi tout à fait sérieux.

Translator. – M. Sollers would like to come back to the political effect of Joyce's writing and more specifically of *Finnegans Wake.* He just wants to know – and he says almost everybody here speaks English and he speaks French, which makes him feel like an oppressed minority – the question he would like to put is, do you realize that since this book, *Finnegans Wake,* has been written, the English language doesn't exist any more ? And yet everybody is going to go on for a very long time speaking a language that doesn't exist, just as the Catholic Church went on speaking Latin. So we have a very important political issue, we have a very small number of living languages, and a huge number of dead languages. He will compare that situation with that of Dante in the fourteenth century. We know that Joyce and other writers in the same period were very interested in Dante. In order to understand the depth of Joyce's work, we have to understand that this goes far back into the past. This is in a way what Engels understood well when he said that the fact of passing from Latin to Italian was a significant revolutionary step : he said in a way this was foreshadowing the arrival of capitalism. Dante represents the first great revolution, which was not only an economic revolution but which consists in changing languages. This is why Joyce, when people discussed politics with him, didn't want to discuss politics in that way because he felt that the way people discussed politics completely separated economics from language (style). And that is why Joyce insisted on the importance of his work and went so far as to say that it's better to pay attention to *Finnegans Wake* than to the invasion of Czechoslovakia. The real, important question is, why do people discuss politics, and why – in doing so – do they use a dead langage ? Because the very important things at stake in Joyce's work are also significant in Marxism, for example in the discussions in Lukács and Brecht. But it seems as always the language of dogmatism remained prevalent.

M. Sollers says he is trying to explain what Joyce tried to do : to declare war against the national language. He said he would fight this war until the end. That is, in a way he based his work on a language that had disappeared – Gaelic. He wanted to destroy an official, imposed language – English. Doing that, he wanted to reach all language. Why did he want to achieve his own revolution by using the maximum possible number of languages ? To show that the end of nationalities had been decided. And this is a political act which has a very strong impact.

Another aspect is that he wanted to reach the unconscious. So if you remain attached to one national language, in that way you remain in the preconscious. That is why great numbers of people who only speak one language are enclosed and refuse on the one side the unconscious and on the other side internationalism. Joyce wants to destroy nationalism, but he wants to go further than internationalism. What he is building with his book is trans-nationalism. Because the language spoken by internationalism is also that of dead languages.

What is his real political action ? He is going to dismember, analyze, go through, re-articulate, annihilate, the maximum cultural, ideological, historical, mythological, linguistic, and religious residues. His most important political act is the way he obstinately tried to analyse religion. If we take religion as, according to Freud, the most important neurotic phenomenon of our civilization, we have to consider that apart from Joyce, nobody has been able to get out of the religious state. Why did he manage to do that ? The reason would be that through his writing he managed to achieve sexual knowledge of our species. Joyce has the same ambition as Freud : he wants to analyze 2 000 years of humanity, and not only concentrate on ten years of politics. This is why Freud's activity was also political, and Fascism always understood that. The first books that are forbidden are Freud's. *Finnegans Wake* is the most important anti-Fascist book written between the two World Wars, at a time when Fascism was gaining throughout Europe. What a Fascist leader does is destroyed by such writing, because it destroys all ideologies. So this book is the strongest action that has been taken against political paranoia. That's why it's both a very amusing and a very serious book.

Fiedler. − I think the remarks we've just heard have raised a key political issue to us − in an ironical setting, because as we were talking about trans-nationalism, M. Sollers was talking at me in French, and I am responding to him in English. Neither of those languages is alas dead for us.

There is one fundamental political error which Joyce made in his work in terms of political analysis of the world which is an error which you have been enchanted by Joyce and other things to share. What Joyce did not understand is that nationalism would indeed remain the sole dynamic political force in the world in the decades and centuries which lay ahead of him. Joyce's *Ulysses* for instance is a study of two nationalist movements which he treats as dead, neither of which in fact *is* dead : the nationalist aspiration of the Jews − Zionism, which is shaking one half of the world right now − and the nationalist aspiration of the Irish, which at the present moment has split Ireland. As a political prophet, Joyce is simply wrong, wrong, wrong. Since I myself grew up as a young man sharing Joyce's illusions and thought that internationalism would be the politics of the future, it's a shock to me to realize that it in fact is the politics of the past, and there is something essentially therefore nostalgic and reactionary in the art of James Joyce.

Compared to Dante, which is the comparison you began by making, Joyce takes the counter-revolutionary activity. Dante began with a world in which there was a sacred language with internationalist aspirations, and when he finishes he insists that people talk the *lingua materna* : not the holy language, but the real language spoken by actual human beings in the streets at each other – by mothers to children, by children to each other. Joyce's attempt to build a holy language has not succeeded in destroying religion and establishing freedom. It's succeeded in destroying the religion with which he was brought up and creating instead a church of high culture, a religion of literature. And not the English language or the French language or the Russian language or for that matter Hebrew or Irish are dead languages, but the language of *Finnegans Wake* is a dead language which is only discussed in tiny circles of people who engage in analysis in a language which itself becomes remoter and remoter from the language of ordinary people, because finally the essential politics of Joyce is the politics of modernism, the politics of elitism, the politics of formalism, the kind of politics which creates a literature which whatever message it contains will not get that message to the world because it goes unread, because it no longer communicates directly to masses of men in the world. From time to time Joyce triumphs over his own modernist politics and aesthetics, but more usually Joyce is the victim of that.

The language which is a dead language is – alas, because it's such a beautiful language – the language of *Finnegans Wake,* that old church Slavonic. And it's studied by scholars and exegetes. The languages which continue are the languages in which the struggles of Ireland are being fought at the present moment, between the North and South of Ireland, and in which struggles are being fought in the Middle East to decide the political state of that world. It's a pity that Joyce, who began in some ways engaged with trying to speak the language of men to men, began to speak a private language to a private cult group. And although I have the profoundest sympathy with the notion of destroying that neurotic area which you call religion, there is no purpose in substituting for it the art-religion. Or culture-religion.

Deane. – There's a story from the Mexican revolution by Carlos Fuentes about the fact that when the peasantry during the Zapata Revolution finally took over the mansions of those whom they regarded as their aristocratic oppressors, what amazed them most in those mansions was the sight of themselves in mirrors, which they had never seen before. They had never seen themselves before. Now Fuentes says this is a kind of little emblem story, in that it produces for us in a capsule form what nationalism always produces : that is, a country that has been colonialized becomes nationalistic and achieves, or tries to achieve, a sense of identity. But the Irish situation, of which Joyce is one of the supreme manifestations, has always been, especially in literature but also in everyday life, one in which you achieve that identity in the mirror of your oppressor. And I would say that Joyce had to smash that mirror and then reconstitute it, but when he reconstituted that mirror it did not reflect any longer the uncreated conscience of his race. It reflected James Joyce, alone. Superb, but still alone. And it could reflect nothing else, because the rest of Ireland had become a ghost. And ghosts don't reflect, as you know.

Fiedler. – In *Ulysses* it reflected Shakespeare, you remember.

Beja. – I wonder if Madame Jolas would like to respond to the sense of Joyce as an elitist.

Jolas. – Well I'd like to respond to a great many things to tell you the truth.

Beja. – Well we'd like you to.

Jolas. – But first of all I think the word nationalism does not describe what is going on in Ireland today, if you'll excuse me. I think it's a remnant, a relic of colonialism, and that it will only be solved through the entire withdrawal probably of the colonizing country, and its army and its soldiers, and so forth. I'm not Irish, but if you will allow me that's my impression.

I also think that a word that has not been pronounced today should be pronounced, which is « regionalism ». I said to a man the other day apropos of something that I was trying to do in connection with the Portuguese events, I said can you help me with this – well it was just sending out announcements, to tell you the truth – and he said no I'm very preoccupied, very busy with my own affair, which is Brittany. And if he's asked, are you French ? he says non, je suis breton. Bon. Well you're laughing, but a lot of that is going on. And I to a certain extent understand it, because I was brought up in Kentucky, and I know that Kentucky felt very different from the United States, and that Virginia even felt more different shall we say, and that Kentucky and Virginia were not exactly the same things. My mother said that she had never become accustomed to Kentucky, because she'd been brought up in Virginia, and so forth. In other words, regionalism is what interested and attracted and you might say convinced Joyce. And which would explain the fact that anybody who came from Dublin, anybody who could talk to him about Dublin, if he could hear the Dublin sound in his ear, and he never lost it... I call that regionalism, not nationalism. Nor was Joyce an internationalist, which in my opinion has become an outworn term like many others.

I'm not at all impressed by the expression that he was not interested in politics, that he was interested in style; I have the impression of somebody who had walked so much faster than the others, that he got there first, and he had to sit down and wait for a long, long time for the others to come along. In other words, if we read Joyce's early writings, and thanks to Richard Ellmann and I forget the other who kindly did so, they have been collected – when they were written in Italian they've even been retranslated – so that we do know that here was a young man who was fantastically politically conscious of what was going on around him.

Apropos of the Vatican, you remember in *Eminent Victorians,* Strachey speaks of Cardinal Newman, I think it was, who went to Rome, and he got the ear of the Vatican and then, comments Strachey, he found it a very dirty ear. Well I think Joyce had the ear of local and international politics very young. He understood perfectly what was going on, and he found it a very dirty ear. And he decided that he would put everything he had to say on that subject in his work, which is what he did.

Now in my association with the man, of course the politics that was going on, shall we say, the rise of Nazism, the antisemitism, all of those things, they hardly seemed – between people who saw a great deal of each other, and understood each other well – they hardly seemed you know to need comment almost. I do remember, however, that in the summer of 1940, when the first copies of a French paper arrived, at St. Gérand-le-Puy, where we were living at the time, he looked at the paper and he said, oh, anti-semitism, that's the easiest of all prejudices to foment. That was the only time I every heard him say anything about that, except once when a young man wrote him a letter from Harvard after the publication of *Ulysses* and said that he wanted to tell him how much he admired his work and so forth, but Mr. Joyce, it makes me very sad to see with what dislike you speak of the Jews. I speak with dislike of the Jews ? said Joyce. He could hardly believe the accusation. And obviously, it was an absolutely unfounded accusation.

I would like to just give one or two more incidents of Joyce's political comments. First of all, I have noted here – as one of the things that I would like to point out – Joyce's extraordinary sense of the antiquity of the human animal. How *old* we are. What an *old* race we are. You remember he said somewhere in one of his earlier books, for the umpteenth time Columbus discovered America in 1492. You remember. And little by little the other times are now coming to light. We are realizing that Columbus did not discover America, as it were. Apropos of the unkind cuts that he received from the Communists – I think it was in 1936 wasn't it ? – from speeches made at the Soviet Writers' Congress held in, no it was 1934, I beg your pardon : Karl Radek wrote, " James Joyce considers that it is the task of the artist to photograph the dunghill through a microscope with a movie camera. Joyce believes that the truth must be shown exactly as it is registered by the movie camera. That is, one movement after the other, whether they be the movements of thoughts or of persons, and out of this eventually will come a great painting. But does Joyce give us a true film representation of life ? No " Karl Radek. Well Joyce said apropos of the dislike of the communists, I don't see why they dislike me. Then he added with a smile, Nobody in my books has any money.

On the other hand, I'm not going to say that he repaid the communists' dislike, I don't think he did, I just think that what he saw going on in eastern, shall we say in Soviet Russia, didn't convince him, and in 1936, I remember, he was asked to give a signed copy of *Ulysses* to a collection that was being taken up in connection with the Spanish War. Well, he didn't give it. In other words, I think he weighed the entire situation, and he didn't want to be particularly identified with that side, shall we say.

Now I should just like to read one note which in my opinion about sums up the position of Joyce. And I think he has really taught us a lot. And if he has taught us something, it seems to me that when things are old and when they no longer correspond to our needs, we should have the honesty to say so and be willing to wait and see what those needs are going to be. So I am going to quote from an article that was written by his close friend, whom I have called elsewhere his alter ego, Paul Léon. Paul Léon as you know was a sociologist, and a lawyer. And he was writing here a criticism of Cole's book on the subject of Guild Socialism. And he ends it on the following note which I think is really applicable to our problems of the day. I'm sure Philippe Sollers would agree with me that here in France, for instance, there is a very interesting political discussion going on. New analyses are being made of old systems. And in the meantime new applications of those old systems are taking place before our very eyes. I'm speaking now of Italy and Portugal. And the news from Italy is extremely interesting, and you might say perhaps new. Here is what Paul Léon writes; I have it in English since I'm speaking English : " there is a page in *Thus Spake Zarathustra* that contains great poetic eloquence as well as philosophical insight. Its essential passage is the following : Evening is coming on and Zarathustra pauses at the entrance to the forest. He is sad. Finally turning to his disciples he says : The sun is long since down. The field is damp. From the woods comes a breath that chills. An unknown something around me is gazing at me thoughtfully. What ? You're still alive, Zarathustra ? Why ? For what ? Through what ? Whither ? Where ? How ? Is it not folly to still be alive ? Ah, my friends, it is evening that questions thus in me. Forgive me my sadness. It is evening now. Forgive me that it should now be evening. Here we see the master (now here I'm quoting Paul Léon), the superman prey to the same anguish as the rest of mankind. He excuses himself that it should now be evening. But we can neither forgive nor condemn him, for the reason that we neither condemn nor forgive the fall of night. This is one of the given facts of human nature against which we can do nothing. Also, if evening induces sadness, no organization, no doctrine can find a remedy for it ". And Paul Léon continues – and almost I think I can say that Joyce would agree with this – " and indeed if we study the most modern social doctrines we would appear to be approaching the evening of our thought. Revolutionary impulse and enthusiasm, faith, if only in a myth capable of recreating this enthusiasm, seem to have run dry. A conscious realism has killed the revolutionary impetus, and today a new, more serious atmosphere reigns in the inner circles of these doctrines where their formulators are only too conscious of the limitations that life itself sets to the realization of ideas. Beside these accepted facts, how hollow and mistaken the proud ringing assertions of triumphant collectivism seem today ".

Here I would like to open a parenthesis and say that Paul Léon was writing this in 1931 I think, and certain events in the Far East had not yet taken place. " Also, how much more sincere, more real and more serious, even though they be more sad, are the conclusions of the modern systems, however tainted with relativism. What they seek to determine is the actual movement, the inevitable evolution, the necessary development of social organization. It is here in fact that political doctrines go hand in hand with scientific thought. And today when we proclaim the inadequacy of the law, spontaneous regulation of social existence, independent development of institutions, the primacy of the rational social legality over that of the organized group, the same thoughts and the same misgivings always come to light. Over and beyond organized and so to speak palpable society, what we seek to discover is the real society with its ineluctable features ".

And I think Joyce was extremely aware of that, and therefore he proposed no system, and he was willing to wait and believe that his faith in humanity... and he did love humanity, there's no doubt about that. *Finnegans Wake* itself is an act of love of humanity. Because it is the Finnegans that are going to wake. And I think that if we can absorb that lesson from Joyce, he will at least have taught us something. And I don't agree with Leslie Fiedler that Joyce's is a dead language and only interesting to scholars and so forth and so on. The number of people that are here today is to me so astounding, having seen the lonely Joyce in the '20's, that I would like to thank all of you for having come and giving the lie to that, that's not true.

Beja. – I'd like just to state the obvious and say that the gratitude is ours. Would anybody else like to respond either to that or to something else that has been said or to ask a particular question ?

Member of audience. – Is it true that Freud's books were the first to be banned by Fascism ?

Sollers. – Le premier ? Je n'ai pas dit le premier. Je dis qu'en tout cas aucun régime fasciste n'a pu laisser s'implanter la pensée de Freud. En tout cas, Freud a été interdit en Allemagne très vite. Il a été obligé de s'exiler en Angleterre où il est mort. Tout récemment, on a brûlé des livres de Freud à Santiago du Chili. Il y a des livres de Freud qui sont interdits par les régimes fascistes.

Je n'ai pas dit le premier.

Translator. – The first ? I didn't say the first. I say in any case that no Fascist regime can tolerate Freud's teaching. Anyway, Freud was banned in Germany very quickly. He had to flee to England. Some of his books have recently been burned in Chile. Freud's books are banned by Fascist regimes.

Robert Boyle, in audience. – Murray, I think it's possible that Joyce was using the word style there in the context of Oscar Wilde, and that he meant by it what Oscar Wilde did, the expression of the self, the reaching down deeper, somewhat as Hopkins in his Purcell sonnet speaks of Purcell's music as expressing those things that can't be expressed in any other way except through the mysterious alchemy of music. I think maybe Joyce had that in mind when he set up his dichotomy. I know it's a dichotomy with politics, but I think it's an inclusive affair that would include politics; I think what he thinks is what Mr. Deane said, he says I'm getting not international but I'm getting sub-personal. In other words, by style meaning I want to express just that which shows my own deepest human experience, and out of that build my literature, and I don't have an interest therefore in the plans of others for social activity, however valuable they may be in other contexts, or to non-artists, or something of that kind, or even to non-Jesuits and non-Catholics, who are also included in his sub-personal — as I understand it and somewhat in opposition to Leslie Fiedler — notion of dead religions. I think Joyce's work expresses his own person, and only that. So that I am somewhat in opposition to Berni — Berni's position I guess I'm getting at in *Finnegans Wake* was that the dreamer is Leopold Bloom. I don't know if Berni still holds to that.

Benstock. — No, it was L. Boom.

Boyle. — L. Boom is far better, since he was a noise in the street and thus gets down to God Himself. But at any rate, all I really wanted to say was that when he said I'm not interested in politics, but in style, he meant that I'm interested in I, which is at the base of everything.

Beja. — Well, if it's a question of Joyce's own personal reaction, how do *we* react — to get to one of his characters — for example, to Stephen Dedalus's refusal in the *Portrait* to sign the petition about the peace conference ? How do we as readers respond to that act ?

Deane. Let me respond by saying that the kind of solipsism you meet in Joyce, and in fact the kind of solipsism you have in the novels between 1880 and the 1920's — the kind of novels that have the artist as hero — that itself is a profound political phenomenon, because that kind of solipsism creates this distinction between the enclosed arena of the self and the noisy arena of politics. That itself is a measure of a political shift in consciousness. It's a measure of a shift in consciousness which Joyce furthered and extended, and which we still in a way suffer from — and I use the word advisedly. We suffer from it in this sense, that once that shift took place it was no longer possible to speak of literature as being a cognitive thing, a thing that had to do with consciousness and truth, right and wrong. Literature became a brilliant form of performance. I think he had a series of systems and structures. The detail of those systems and structures could identify by its code a particular culture, identify a particular author. But the phenomenon, the radical phenomenon below that performance was that literature had in fact separated itself disdainfully from a public world as a world which was no longer prone to, which was no longer liable to the systems of order which the imagination in the area of performance could create. And it seems to me a matter of that, self and order.

Benstock. — The easy assumption for the reader to make is that Stephen is objecting to pacifism. The assumption that Cranly and Davin and MacCann make is that there is something personally obnoxious and difficult and stubbornly perverse about Stephen. The extended assumption that perhaps we should make is that Stephen has a political sophistication that rises above the actual document, and that he might suspect that the document promulgated by the Czar of the Russias may not be legitimately and sincerely and politically, pragmatically, a really pacifistic document. To that extent, I see a greal deal of sophistication in that very political situation in *Portrait*. And perhaps the same distinction exists – it is Stanislaus Joyce who causes the comment that we've been discussing, and you notice if Joyce just drops a comment, how much we can do with it – perhaps the distinction is between Stanislaus Joyce's politics and James Joyce's style. And if that distinction is the real one, as political as I consider myself, I think I would choose James Joyce's style. And I think that Philippe Sollers has very definitely indicated why I would make that choice.

Jolas. – I just want to say that I think it's very dangerous to always identify everything Stephen did or said with James Joyce.

Richard Kain, in audience. – I wonder if it would be in order at this time to congratulate the members of this panel. I think it's a true symposium.

Arnold Goldman, in audience. – I would like to observe something about the kind of post-Parnell thought which I believe is rightly seen in each of Joyce's first three works. I would attribute this to the extent that I see Joyce's characters making this kind of attribution about Irish society. I do not hold Joyce necessarily responsible for leaving Padraic Pearse out of the characters. Arthur Griffith, we know, walks in and goes dancing out again. But it seems to me that we're asking something very strange of our literature if we insist that Joyce should have discovered real revolutionary trends as he could have done by 1922. It seems to me that Joyce says something very accurate about certain people's self-attribution and their ideas about Irish politics. I don't see why you seem to be asking him to go one step further and dissociate himself by a kind of narrative fiat from a view of Irish society that he creates for a group of people to have.

Beja. – We have about five more minutes for just a few essential questions.

[At this point Nuala O'Faolain responded from the audience to Mr. Goldman, but unfortunately she was too far back in the hall for the microphone to be able to pick up her words.]

William M. Chace, in audience. – With all deference to Mme. Jolas' warm and affectionate memories of James Joyce, it seems to me that I recall a mournful and melancholy silence falling upon this room when you remarked about Joyce's response to Nancy Cunard's request that he lend his name to the work against Spanish Fascism. Joyce in that case as he was on many political occasions was at most indifferent. I think by that quotation, by that memory...

Jolas. – Not indifferent. But aware of what was involved in the Spanish War. And it was not indifference, I assure you.

Chace. – Yes, I'm sure he was quite aware. He was aware of many things, he was a very well read man. But I think that in your memory you've struck upon a chord of memories of all of us associated with Joyce, that he was in many cases seeking always to rise to a perspective above and beyond. And I quote from – peharps it's a passage in Ellmann's book that all of us know, but I think it might be worth mentioning. It begins :

> ...he cultivated disengagement, and remarked one night at dinner at Paul Léon's, 'Isn't this Hitler a phenomenon ? Think of getting a whole people behind you.' Nora picked up a knife and said 'You stop that, Jim.' He spoke highly of German precision to friends whom he knew to be hostile to any favorable mention of Germany. Samuel Beckett spoke to Joyce of the Nazi persecution of the Jews, but Joyce pointed out there had been similar persecutions before. It was not that he condoned them, but that he wished to withdraw to another perspective. When Jacques Mercanton asked him to contribute something to *Mass und Werk,* Joyce at first agreed, then remembered that Thomas Mann had stated his anti-Nazi position there in 1937, and said, 'No, the review is politically oriented.' He did not wish *Finnegans Wake* to be banned by any country because of its author's supposed political bias.

It seems to me that in most respects Joyce's politics were a perfectly esoteric and a perfectly removed politics, useless to our time and useless to his own. I don't see this as a particularly bad thing or as a particularly good thing, I see it as a particularly Joycean thing. And without a bad attitude and in the strange harmony of all the rest of his attitudes, his genius most happily prospered. So be it.

To get a sense of his apolitical stance, his disengagement from politics, one need make only a casual reference to the right and to the left of political memory. By comparison we have Wyndham Lewis, Pound, and Eliot on the extreme right : those politics were authentic politics, and in some cases they had a real, genuine effect upon those writers and upon certain people around them. Or, to move to the left, we have Brecht, we have in the United States Upton Sinclair, we have if you will Albert Maltz, we have John Steinbeck, we have Clara Weatherwax. All of those people are also political, but that should indicate something about Joyce's politics, for they were politics in truly Joycean ways – that is truly bizarre, as I say, esoteric and useless ways. The question that strikes me as being perfectly appropriate to this panel is why it is that a good many of us here would wish, against much evidence to the contrary, to push Joyce to the left. Professor Henke began by remarking upon conditions in American campuses, and it would indeed be pleasing to go back and tell our undergraduates that Joyce was a good guy just like we are good guys and stood for the good things. Well he didn't. Now we have to live with that, but for me it's a comfortable living. He was a genius.

Benstock. – Incidentally, we've been told we don't have to end in five minutes. We can take another ten or fifteen.

Beja. – Okay, would you like to respond to that ?

Henke. – I'm speechless. I think we all read Joyce a bit differently. Perhaps this is one indication of the solipsistic way we are all reading Joyce, because we do have such different interpretations, even of the political dimensions of his work. And of course it's become a kind of cliché to say an apolitical stance is also a political position.

Beja. – I'd like just to react a little bit. [To Mr. Chace]. It seems to me that Joyce's record seems pretty good if the comparison to be made is the comparison to those names that you brought out. Then he stands up very well, and not just as a writer but as a thinker, and as a political thinker.

Jolas. – I should like to recall my figure of speech, of the race that he had run and that he was waiting for us at the end of the race. And that we had much to learn from what he had learned while he ran that race.

[Here Morton Levitt spoke from the audience, but his words were not clearly picked up by the tape recorder].

Benstock. – Perhaps the operative word for the title and a very important word is perspectives, rather than politics. But I'm rather horrified by that quotation from the biography. I'm horrified that it is being used as documentary evidence. It is anecdotal, it is misleading, I want to know the tone in which that was said, the circumstances, the context, Joyce's degree of personal disgruntlement. The easy, clever, quippish sort of thing that makes a biography highly readable to me is not evidence of a political perspective.

Member of audience. – I'm surprised that nobody has thought of Joyce as a political consultant. I would be delighted to live in the New Bloomusalem.

Benstock. – This is it.

Henke. – Bloom is also the first person to suggest a guaranteed minimal income, so he got ahead of Sweden by about fifty years.

Sollers. – Moi, je voudrais dire que je suis un peu étonné qu'on ne discute pas de l'effet politique de ce qu'écrit Joyce. Lorsque *Ulysses* est interdit par la censure en Angleterre à cause du monologue de Molly Bloom, il y a un effet politique. La position de Joyce par rapport à la sexualité est politique, surtout quand on connaît le puritanisme anglo-saxon. Et peut-être c'est bon qu'un français le dise.

Translator. – Philippe Sollers wants to say that he is surprised that nobody has yet been discussing the political effects of Joyce's writing. When *Ulysses* is banned in England because of Molly Bloom's soliloquy, that is a political effect. His position concerning sexuality is a political one, especially when one considers Anglo-Saxon puritanism. And it's perhaps a good thing that it's a Frenchman who should mention that.

Beja. – Would anybody want to conjecture what the nonexistent chapter in Kate Millett's *Sexual Politics* would have been like, had there been one devoted to Joyce ? Would it have been an attack, do you think ?

Henke. – We're going to discuss that on Friday, in the panel on Joyce's women.

Sollers. – Je veux dire simplement que personne n'a mieux analysé que Joyce en quoi la famille pouvait être le noyau éventuel d'une répression générale qui peut s'étendre à toute la société. Et on appelle ça le fascisme.

Translator. – No one better than Joyce has analyzed how the family can become the center of a general repression which can affect all society. And that is called Fascism.

Julia Holloway, in audience. – I would like to add to the comment that was made by Seamus, on the cracked mirror, the smashed mirror. When it is broken, it can reflect opposites, and M. Sollers brought up Dante, and said that this was an anti-Fascist work. Alas, Dante was used by Fascists, as part of their Fascist dream. I think it very important for us who have a responsibility as critics not to allow that to happen to Joyce. And here I quite disagree with Mr. Fiedler, because I do feel that *Finnegans Wake* counteracts the capitalism of *Ulysses*. I like the liberation immensely of Molly Bloom's politics, all of these things. But I sense that they have their own built-in dangers. One must indulge in them for a while and then go beyond them, for transfiguration. Because each struggle, dispossession, the selling of one's birthright for a mess of pottage, is what is at the crux of *Finnegans Wake*. And I think it's in that that we find the battle between the sexes, between the races, and between the religions.

Member of audience. – I'd like to add some emphasis to what Seamus Deane has said in the first place, and this is to stress that the thing called colonialism is of massive importance in interpreting Joyce's work. What it made impossible for him, I believe, is the simple reductive approach towards the material. There is no single political program in Joyce. There's no possibility of using Joyce's language to describe our intention to refute a society. It is exactly in the nature of this particular form of narrative that he represents the society's antinomies as irresolvable, in terms of a single synthesis, and they can only be described in terms of systematizations... Such a system makes solutions of a political order impossible. But there is a sound political dimension to Joyce, and this is the fact that he's continually preoccupied with the city, what it is, and what it is to live in the city. Consider what he does with the motto of the city of Dublin, *Obedientia civium urbis felicitas*.

So there's a profound consciousness of the strategy, of the alienation, which is part of the life of all urban dwellers, and especially urban dwellers in colonial

Ireland. I think James Joyce beats minds like Frantz Fanon in modern times in his description of a multi-rationale in place of a single rationale. What I imagine that political figures writing in contemporary journalism are attempting to do is to describe the world or the future in terms of a single program. The spirit of Joyce is absolutely opposed to that.

Beja. − I would like not to overstay our welcome, and I think it is time we closed. I'd like to thank you for coming and to remind you that in the *Portrait* little Stephen Dedalus remembers Dante telling him that Parnell was a bad man. And he wonders if they were still talking about that at home. That was called politics. They're still talking about that at home and it's still called politics. Thank you.

Morris BEJA
Ohio State University

Joyce and the other arts

" Aeolus » and the Technique of Collage

(Abstract)

The " Aeolus » episode of *Ulysses* − to which Joyce added a series of newspaper headlines and captions as the novel went to press − is one of the earliest instances in modern fiction of the application of the principles of collage to narrative technique. As developed by the Cubists and Futurists, collage was a synthetic technique of art involving diverse materials variously arranged and applied to cardboard, wood, and canvas. One of these materials was the newspaper clipping − in particular the headline or caption. In Cubist collage the headlines and captions generally served no purpose beyond contributing to the over-all composition an aura of contemporaneity (or sometimes its very opposite), but in Futurist collage they frequently functioned more directly to comment on the subject of the picture, the aims of the Futurist group, or the aims of art in general. It is in this last connection that we see most clearly a link between collage as it was developed in the early years of the twentieth century and the art of Joyce in " Aeolus " : the headlines or captions of " Aeolus " serve to comment on the events of the chapter and the purposes of art in general, in such a way that one wonders whether Joyce's addition of the headlines and captions did not reflect the influence of collage or collage-inspired poetry like that of the Futurist or Cubist poets. There are headlines or captions which satirize the action, and also those that comment on Stephen's artistic decisions and Joyce's earlier manner as a fictionist. These in turn have their analogues in the work of the collagists of the 'teens and 'twenties. An additional element of connection is what might be termed the collage technique in stream-of-consciousness prose : that is, the use of the part for the whole, of the fragment for the entire unit, throughout *Ulysses* (though especially in the earlier episodes) as throughout collage. This last − since it involves not merely headlines and captions but a whole narrative strategy − takes us beyond technical considerations to considerations of aesthetic wholes.

Archie LOSS
Pennsylvania State University

Joyce and Surrealism

(Abstract)

One can easily isolate points of comparison between Joyce and surrealism, but it would be inaccurate and misleading to say that Joyce was influenced by the Surrealists, despite his evocation of the dream state in Nighttown, despite his wholesale unleashing of the unconscious in *Finnegans Wake.*

Philippe Sollers, in his address at this conference, talked of Joyce's destruction of language, and thus of consciousness, in *Finnegans Wake,* a work which reaches us on the level of preconscious activity. In terms of this destruction one might call *Finnegans Wake* an example of Dada art, for the Dadaists, recoiling against war and the society which permitted it, the technology which advanced it, sought to destroy communication, to destroy art itself. Thus we have Duchamp's upside down urinal, labelled " Fountain ", an example of found art; we have Tzara's lists of words called poems. The role of the artist *qua* artist is denied; there is neither imagination nor even fancy in Dada.

The element of *hazard* − chance − was important to the Surrealists as well, notably in their experiments with automatic writing. But although they swore that this was the way in which their works were created, I think that we must question them as much as we do Joyce's fables about his own work; they are traps to seduce the unwary reader. We are wiser to accept Anna Balakian's premise that automatic writing was to Surrealist art as " the practice of scales to the musician " (*Surrealism : The Road to the Absolute,* p. 146) − necessary exercises preceding the finished work.

Certainly Joyce would repudiate the Surrealists' rejection of the artist's control. What he would accept was the Surrealist attempt to enter man's unconscious and to convey that state in art. André Breton, in " The First Manifesto of Surrealism ", attacks the realistic novel with its interminable detail of man's exterior life but with no revelation of his inner life; Joyce attacks the realistic novel by means of his hyper-realism and, of course, his stream of consciousness.

One could extend the list of parallels between Joyce and the Surrealists : their collage was certainly an important structural device for him; *le merveilleux,* so highly vaunted by Breton, is not unlike Joyce's epiphany; both Joyce and the Surrealists make much use of humor, of playfulness in language, of dream as central to man's life. They can also be compared in their opposing treatment of love, of woman, of the child within us.

A mere list is superficial; more valuable, I think, is the recognition that Joyce's art is most like that of the Surrealists in their growth beyond Dada : they were concerned not with destroying art but with its revitalization, not with disembodying art but with a restoration of its humanity. Certainly we see this in *Ulysses* and even, I think, in its total scheme rather than its discrete parts, in *Finnegans Wake* as well.

Annette S. LEVITT
Temple University

Everyman blooms as everybody

Adaline Glasheen suggests (*A WN,* XIII.1 (Feb. 1976), 16) that the revival of *Everyman* in London during the summer of 1901 sparked the imagination of Joyce " with future possibilities of Bloom and Here Comes Everybody ". Might I also suggest that he received similar inspiration from a lesser known play by a dramatist popular in his youth to whom he refers in one of the critical pieces.

José Echegaray y Eizaguirre (1832-1916) was one of the most popular and most respected Spanish dramatists of the 19th century and the co-winner, with Frédéric Mistral, of the Nobel Prize for Literature in 1904. In the 90's he was widely read and translated, and his works were performed both in Europe and in America. Joyce refers to him in his pamphlet of 1901, " The Day of the Rabblement ", in the same sentence in which he refers to *Pelléas et Mélisande.* Speaking of the taste of the multitude that comprised the audience of the Irish Literary Theatre, Joyce remarks : " ... the rabblement, placid and intensely moral, is enthroned in boxes and galleries amid a hum of approval – *la bestia Trionfante* – and those who think that Echegaray is 'morbid', and titter coyly when Mélisande lets down her hair, are not sure but they are the trustees of every intellectual and poetic treasure " (1). Joyce may merely have been repeating someone else's phrase, but he may actually have known at least a portion of what was probably the best-known of Echegaray's plays.

The Irish Literary Theatre and its successor the Abbey apparently never performed Echegaray (2), but a great many other theaters did, including, in Paris, the Symbolist Théâtre de L'Œuvre of Aurélien-Marie Lugné-Poë, the actor and director to whom, years later, Joyce was to submit for consideration the manuscript of *Exiles* (3). The play included in the small group of Spanish and Italian works performed by the Théâtre de L'Œuvre was the one that Joyce may have known – *El Gran Galeoto,* first performed in Madrid in 1881.

The title of the play comes from the reference to Galleot in Francesca's tale in the *Inferno,* but refers, as we learn in scene V of Act II from Ernest (the adopted son), to the " entire social mass ", which has influenced Don Julian (an old man) to believe that Teodora (his young wife) and Ernest have become lovers under Don Julian's roof and which, furthermore, has influenced Teodora and Ernest finally to become lovers, if not in fact at least in spirit : " Sometimes it is the entire social mass that is Galeoto. It then unconsciously exercises the office under the

(1) *The Critical Writings of James Joyce,* ed. Ellsworth Mason and Richard Ellmann, New York, 1964, p. 70.

(2) See Andrew Malone, *The Irish Drama,* London, 1929; rpt. 1965, Appendix III, p. 335.

(3) For the performance record of the Théâtre de L'Œuvre, see Jacques Robichez, *Le Symbolisme au théâtre : Lugné-Poë et les débuts de L'Œuvre,* Paris, 1957, Annexe III, p. 506.

influence of a vice of quite another aspect, but so dexterously does it work against honour and modesty that no greater Galeoto can ever be found " (53) (4).

The story of Ernest and Teodora occurs within the half-frame provided by the Prologue to the play (there is no epilogue or other corresponding section at the end). It is this Prologue that interests us chiefly here. Ernest is attempting to write a play and, in a sense, the play that he is attempting to write and that he describes to Don Julian is the play we actually see. In the second scene he tells Don Julian : " When I first conceived the idea I imagined it full of promise, but when I attempt to give it form, and vest it in an appropriate stage garb, the result shows something extraordinary, difficult, undramatic and impossible " (5). The principal character cannot appear on stage – not, as Don Julian first thinks, because he is ugly or repugnant or bad or too gigantic, but because he is – everybody (5). Ernest describes his character further : " Look ! Each individual of this entire mass, each head of this monster of a thousand heads, of this Titan of the century, whom I call *everybody,* takes part in my play for a flying moment, to utter but one word, fling a single glance. Perhaps his action in the tale consists of a smile, he appears but to vanish. Listless and absent-minded, he acts without passion, without anger, without guile, often for mere distraction's sake " (6-7) (6). This mass character is to commit an act of evil, but the playwright's " sole pretention is to prove that not even the most insignificant actions are in themselves insignificant or lost for good or evil. For, concentrated by the mysterious influences of modern life, they may reach to immense effects " (7).

The drama that Ernest imagines – in which the principal character is everybody – will involve little external action. As he puts it, " It will be all simple, ordinary, almost vulgar... so that the drama will not have any external action. The drama evolves within the personages : it advances slowly : to-day takes hold of a thought, to-morrow of a heart-beat, little by little undermines the will " (7). Furthermore, the action proper will not begin until the curtain falls. The dismayed Don Julian sums it up :

DON JULIAN : ... A drama in which the chief personage cannot appear; in which there is hardly any love; in which nothing happens but what

---

(4) All citations to the play are to the translation by Hannah Lynch in *The Great Galeoto* and *Folly or Saintliness,* London, 1895.

(5) The Spanish is " todo el mundo ". Echegaray uses the phrase ironically to open his dedication of the play. See José Echegaray, *Teatro escogido,* Madrid, 1959, p. 643.

(6) Cf. " this monster of a thousand heads " (" ese monstruo de cien mil cabezas ") with *" la bestia Trionfante "* of " The Day of the Rabblement ". Cf. also " The hundredheaded rabble of the cathedral close ", *Ulysses* 39 : 37-8.

(7) The ellipsis comes in the text. The word " drama " (or " it " is the subject of the last three phrases. The Spanish text is clearer : " El drama va por dentro de los personajes; avanza lentamente; se apodera hoy de un pensamiento, mañana de un latido del corazón; mina la voluntad poco a poco " (*Teatro escogido,* p. 649).

happens every day; that begins with the fall of the curtain upon the last act, and which has no name. I don't know how it is to be written, still less how it is to be acted, how it is to find an audience, nor how it can be called a drama.

ERNEST : Nevertheless, it is a drama, if I could only give it proper form, and that I can't do. (9-10)

It is clear by now that in this projected drama of Ernest's there are several things of interest to the student of Joyce : one of these is the notion of a character who would sum up in himself everybody, and another is the notion of developing this character not through declamation or exposition, but through what appear to be trifles, actions "simple, ordinary, almost vulgar" – the drama evolving within the minds of the characters. In these notions we may see, in other words, an anticipation of the sort of internal development Joyce was to manage in *Ulysses* and *Finnegans Wake,* and, furthermore, an anticipation of a specific character – HCE.

The idea of a universal drama, or universal work of literature, was not uncommon in the 19th century, particularly among the French Symbolists and those who inspired them. The drama with no external action was specifically a Symbolist notion, carried out, or at least attempted, in the Théâtre de l'Œuvre and elsewhere, and perhaps Echegaray had it in mind when he wrote his Prologue. If Echegaray's play is in any way to carry out Ernest's ideas in the Prologue, it cannot be counted a success, for the evil, though pointless enough, is committed by a handful of specific characters and tends, because they are relatives, to become a family affair. Furthermore, although the blood is shed off stage, there is enough verbal violence on stage to make the atmosphere anything but quiet. If Joyce knew this work, he could not have learned from it much about the process of creating the universal character or the drama of the ordinary, but, as a young man, he might have gained from it a suggestion of the possibility of both.

Archie K. Loss
Pennsylvania State University

Joyce and the other arts

Although I find the early presentations on this panel quite convincing, I still have reservations about the subject of Joyce and the other arts. My comments are somewhat impressionistic − even surreal, perhaps − but they relate to the very realistic issue of Joyce's artistry as a maker of fiction and to our appreciation of that role.

The biographical evidence reveals Joyce's pedestrian taste in painting and suggests that, music aside, he had little real interest in the other arts. (Bloom does, of course, but on such minor matters of taste, he can never serve as our guide; his sensibility is reserved for more significant human concerns). Stephen too, I suspect, has little artistic taste or interest in art, and his aesthetic theory may well be akin to his poetry − offered partly in seriousness, but at least partly parodied (reflecting perhaps Joyce's own ambivalence toward his character).

It is fair, I think, to conclude from this very brief overview − and from the evidence of the fiction itself − that Joyce's models are drawn not from the other arts, not even from such literary forms as the drama, but from the history of the novel itself. His own pretence that Dujardin had served as his source for the perfection of the stream of consciousness (he might have spoken of Debussy or Monet) would seem to indicate Joyce's acknowledgement of this fact. What he did with inherited forms, what he invented himself, is inherently novelistic, not dramatic or musical or derived from the plastic arts.

This may seem a truism, but it is easy to forget in our pleasure at finding foreign analogies : we have much to learn yet about *Ulysses* and *Finnegans Wake* as novels, and we are not likely to learn it, I suspect, if we look elsewhere for our terms and our models, *e.g.,* if we insist on discussing them as " anatomies " and ignore the more familiar but still undeveloped potential of " point of view ". (Maurice Beebe was careful to avoid this trap in relating Impressionism to point of view in *A Portrait*).

The parallels with other arts can obviously be useful, and it is not impossible that we will find evidence of borrowings by and influence on Joyce. But even if we were to find irrefutable proof that Joyce, like Proust, had borrowed and learned from the painters, I would continue to believe that it remains most fruitful to discover his novels in terms of the development of the novel as form − as a development out of earlier novels and as the source of future development.

Morton LEVITT
Temple University

Work after the Wake

Or a first look at Joyce's Influence on Arno Schmidt

sey Mir gepriesen,
Mann aus Du-
blin !

(ZT (1), 988)

Among West German writers of the past thirty years only four may be said to have been influenced by *Finnegans Wake.* Of course narrative techniques like the *monologue intérieur* came to the knowledge of German writers, as can be seen clearly in Alfred Döblin's *Berlin Alexanderplatz,* published in 1929; and as early as 1931 Hermann Broch wrote his famous essay " James Joyce und die Gegenwart ", which was followed fourteen years later by the novel *Der Tod des Vergil* where Broch presents unspoken thoughts extensively. *Ulysses* has left its mark evidently on novels by Uwe Johnson, Martin Walser and Wolfgang Koeppen, to name just a few. But the prose techniques of *Finnegans Wake* have not been widely adopted. There is one Poem by Ernst Jandl, the Viennese poet, which probably owes something to the sudden insight into the revolutionary possibilities of Joyce's way of handling language – the poem " Wien. Heldenplatz ", a very bitter political poem in which Jandl tries to portray the fascist enthusiasm of the people in Vienna at the time of Hitler's conquest of Austria, and, at the same time, the quasi-erotic lasciviousness among the masses hailing him (2).

Then there is, larger in size, the much more extensive work *fa:m ahniesqwow* by Hans G. Helms, published in 1959. As the title with its blending of the words " fama ", " fame ", " foam ", " ahnen ", " Anis ", " Gau ", " wow " and a few others shows, we have a dissolution of normal syntax and a consistent use of

---

(1) *Zettels Traum,* (also, on title page : *Zettel's Traum*), Stahlberg Verlag, Stuttgart. 1970.

(2) Ernst Jandl, " Laut und Luise ". Darmstadt/Berlin 1971 (Sammlung Luchterhand 38), p. 44.

homophony and puns and also, as can be seen when the whole text is read, a dissolution of the narrative plot. Helms was one of the first apprentices of Joyce in West Germany, of the Joyce of the Wake. – And then we have a text by Hans Wollschläger called *Nacht-Stücke,* published two years ago (3), where *Finnegans Wake* can be felt – not very surprising of course in the work of a man who spent four years of his life transplanting *Ulysses* into German (4) and who has also translated, if translated is the word, the " Anna Livia Plurabelle " chapter.

Whereas the texts of Jandl, Helms and Wollschläger have remained a " Geheimtipp " among German literati without drawing much public attention, the author commonly associated with, and compared to (although so far rather superficially), James Joyce is Arno Schmidt, the 62 year old writer whose publishing career began in 1949 and who reached the peak of fame, paradoxically enough, when his monstrous and supersized 1334 page book *Zettels Traum* appeared in 1970. The title would translate into English as, either, " The Dream of a Slip of Paper " or as " Bottom's Dream " (since it alludes to the German version of Bottom the Weaver in *Midsummer Night's Dream*) and so fits into the new tradition of *Finnegans Wake* with good reason. In a comment on his new book, used as a kind of publicity " trailer " and broadcast over the wireless *before* the publication of *ZettelsTraum,* Schmidt himself named *Finnegans Wake* as a kind of counterpart, as something already known, from which however – in spite of praise and basic admiration – he intended to keep some distance in matters of principal importance. The author thus indirectly admitted that the two works have some features in common and that the differences too were fully intended.

The relationship dates back to the year 1957 when Schmidt apparently first read *Ulysses* and immediately launched on a furious attack on the absolutely inadequate (in his opinion) German translation by Georg Goyert (5). In his early novels and stories Schmidt had already used a narrative technique closely related to the *monologue intérieur,* but it seems very probable that Joyce had no part in this early development (though Döblin may have had). The first influences of *Ulysses* and, presumably, *Finnegans Wake* are to be found in Schmidt's novel *Kaff auch Mare Crisium,* of 1960 : the number of violations of orthographic rules, of puns and portmanteau words has risen sharply, and Schmidt begins – still very unsystematically, as if not sure what to do with all these new possibilities – to make use of homophony and homoiophony and other linguistic devices for creating double meaning and double talk in German, a language that does not lend itself to such practices as easily as English. As a little acknowledgement of the apprenticeship there is the " ESSENTIAL JAMES JOYCE " (always spelt in capital letters) lying on the luggage rack of the small car of the hero's girl friend. In

---

(3) Hans Wollschläger, " Nacht-Stücke ". In : *Das Tintenfass,* Diogenes-Taschenbuch 83, Zürich 1974, p. 151-162.

(4) James Joyce, *Ulysses,* 2 vols., Frankfurter Ausgabe 3.1 and 3.2, Frankfurt 1975.

(5) Arno Schmidt, " Ulysses in Deutschland. Kritische Anmerkungen zu einer James-Joyce-Übersetzung ". In : *Frankfurter Allgemeine Zeitung,* 26.10.1957.

1960 and 1961 Schmidt published two pieces of literary criticism on *Finnegans Wake,* documents of a *furor teutonicus,* bent on incorporating the Wake into the realm of literature that Schmidt feels of supreme importance (6). Like these two radio dialogues, another literary " radio feature " commemorating the 25th anniversary of Joyce's death (7) in 1966, shows three distinct characteristics : first, Schmidt didn't really keep up with the results of Joyce scholarship; second, he voiced his dislike of " mystification ", which, in his opinion, had driven Joyce too far into *Finnegans Wake,* so that the breathtaking complexity was an unnecessary performance of *l'art pour l'art* − and yet, at the same time, he displayed an enthusiastic interest in the way Joyce handled language; thirdly, he maintained that research had not paid enough attention to the underlying autobiographical facts : quarrels (out of jealousy) between James and Stanislaus Joyce. Schmidt even went so far as to say that the newly created language of *Finnegans Wake* only served to disguise the libel and slander uttered against the brother, Stanislaus (8).

In the years around 1960 Schmidt intended to translate *Finnegans Wake* into German. In one of the radio dialogues, entitled " Überlegungen zu einer Lesbarmachung von 'Finnegans Wake' ", he presented some 12 pages of Wake passages in German. Despite all objections which can be raised, these passages are ravishingly musical and rhythmical pieces of prose (9). They were to serve as a sort of pilot study for the translation project. There was however no chance of a publisher to advance the means for the three years which Schmidt considered necessary for the translation. But he did translate Stanislaus Joyce's *Dublin Diary* and *My Brother's Keeper* (10). So, on the whole, he is well acquainted with Joyce's life and work, and his own work in the early sixties, especially the short novel *Caliban über Setebos,* bears witness to the compulsion of the language of *Finnegans Wake* as well. This short novel tells the adventures of a poet who, for a few hours, is visiting a village in which he hopes to find a love of his youth again. He indeed meets her but finds her grown a dirty old hag, he flees her in disgust and is almost killed by a band of lesbians whose orgy in an old barn he secretly observed. The background of the myth of Orpheus is reminiscent of the way *Ulysses* uses the *Odyssey :* the poet (Orpheus) travels to the forlorn, fog-enshrouded

---

(6) Arno Schmidt, " Der Triton mit dem Sonnenschirm. Überlegungen zu einer Lesbarmachung von 'Finnegans Wake' ", " Kaleidoskopische Kollidier-Eskapaden ". In : *Der Triton mit dem Sonnenschirm. Grossbritannische Gemütsergetzungen,* Karlsruhe 1969, p. 194-252 and 292-321.

(7) Arno Schmidt, " Das Buch Jedermann. James Joyce zum 25. Todestage ". In : *Der Triton mit dem Sonnenschirm. Grossbritannische Gemütsergetzungen,* Karlsruhe 1969, p. 254-290.

(8) Arno Schmidt, *Der Triton mit dem Sonnenschirm,* p. 289 ff.

(9) *Der Triton mit dem Sonnenschirm,* p. 195 ff. In the meantime a discussion of Schmidt's translations and explications of *Finnegans Wake,* by Fritz Senn, has appeared in *Bargfelder Bote,* Lieferung 27/February 1978.

(10) Stanislaus Joyce, *Meines Bruders Hüter,* Frankfurt 1960. − Stanislaus Joyce, *Das Dubliner Tagebuch des Stanislaus Joyce,* Frankfurt 1964.

village (descends into Hades) to get back his love (Euridike) and is finally pursued by the lesbians (maimed by the priestesses of Bacchus). The language of the story, with almost every word prepared to carry several meanings ("realistic", "mythological", "allusive", etc.), contains, according to Schmidt's own statement, "3000 trills & fiorituras" (11), exploiting all possibilities of changing the spelling of words that make them multidimensional. Like the translations from *Finnegans Wake,* Caliban über Setebos is a wonderfully complex and, at times, very musical piece of prose, and so far philological research has not been able to trace the full meaning of more than a few dozen allusions and neologisms in that story (12).

Between 1964 and 1970 Schmidt published almost nothing new. And soon there were rumours that he was composing his *Work in Progress,* a novel monstrous in size and complexity, *Zettels Traum,* which was at the same time to be a "tractatus psychoanalytico-philologus", an essay on the part played by the unconscious of Edgar Allan Poe in his choice of words, images, metaphors and landscapes in his writings, a result of Schmidt's labour of translating much of Poe's work into German (13), and of his studies of Freud's investigations into the mechanisms of dreams (especially in his *Traumdentung,* 1900). And *Zettels Traum* can be considered the book with which Schmidt entered competition with Joyce's Wake. By the way, *Zettels Traum* contains at least (computation up to now) 220 quotations from and allusions to the work of Joyce, his life and that of his family (14), and *Finnegans Wake* is most frequently quoted from. Many quotations have not of course yet been traced and I suspect that future research will yet yield a rich crop.

On the other hand, as far as the establishing of a correct text is concerned – certainly one of the most urgent tasks of Joyce philology – , we, the Schmidtians, will have no worries whatsoever since the published text of *Zettels Traum* is a full-size photostatic copy of the author's typescript.

The Schmidt scholars in their first attempts with *Zettels Traum* face much the same problems that readers of *Finnegans Wake* had in the years after its first publication. That is to say, we do not as yet know very much about it, especially since there were no advance publications or early fragments before 1970 comparable to the instalments of *Work in Progress* and carefully directed critical leaks in *transition.* Above all, there is nothing in the manner of *Our Exagmination Round His Factification...* of 1929.

There was, as we know, no great fuss about the publication of *Finnegans Wake* in 1939. Quite the contrary in the case of *Zettels Traum,* whose publication

---

(11) Letter to Jörg Drews, 13.9.1964.

(12) Robert Wohlleben, "Götter und Helden in Niedersachsen. Über das mythologische Substrat des Personals in 'Caliban über Setebos'". In : *Bargfelder Bote,* Lieferung 3/June 1973.

(13) Edgar Allan Poe, *Werke I-IV,* translated by Arno Schmidt, Hans Wollschläger, Kuno Schumann and others. Olten/Freiburg, 1966 ff.

(14) Dieter Stündel, *register zu 'Zettels Traum',* München 1974.

was greeted by dozens of small or large reviews in Germany (15). What further stimulated public interest was the surprising publication of a pirated edition by a group of underground printers who probably perpetrated their infringement on copyright in Berlin. This edition (of 1 000 copies) by an unknown (and as yet undiscovered) press offered the novel in somewhat smaller size and at considerably lower price than was the *Ur-Zettel*. In spite of the author's dismay, even the pirate venture contributed to his reputation and helped the sale of all his other books.

Very soon after the publication of the original *Zettels Traum,* in April 1970, the serious philologists and the cross-word puzzle addicts (often combined in one person) among the devoted fans joined in team work for the decipherment of the big book. William York Tindall remembers that as early as 1940 he, " ...to learn more about *Finnegans Wake,* gathered a little group of graduate students at Columbia in the belief that a committee, reading the text, talking it over, and bringing to it a variety of languages and learning, might do more with the book than I [Tindall] alone, with small learning and less Greek " (16). Something analogous happened in Germany. A team of readers gathered and decided to join their efforts to understand the book; two years later these Schmidt fans began to publish their counterpart to *A Wake Newslitter,* a quarterly called *Bargfelder Bote* (Bargfeld Messenger), after the village where Schmidt lives in the Lüneburg Heath. This specialized quarterly has, at the time of this talk, reached its 18th number. It deals with all the works of Schmidt, and several issues have brought first notes on the meaning of words and sentences in *Zettels Traum,* quite similar to the *Wake* glosses. In addition, a first index of important names, ideas and technical terms in *Zettels Traum* is already available. Certainly the *Register zu Zettels Traum : eine Annäherung* by Dieter Stündel, published 1974, is still very insufficient and not without grave flaws, but it is at least a first aid kit for the serious reader.

What Schmidt's readers could discover very soon is that the narrative thread in *Zettels Traum* is much more conspicuous than in *Finnegans Wake.* As to the story that forms the backbone of the book, we are on solid ground, for in most parts we know who says what to whom and in what language. But the plot appears so simple that it becomes obvious this is not what it's all about, and the irritating spelling, the innumerable quotations (open or hidden) and the language in general point to the fact that there is much to discover.

Leaving aside many dark spots and stumbling blocks, even on a first reading of *Zettels Traum* basic orientation is possible. This is the result of a deliberate strategy. Referring to a book whose text was printed in two columns − *Kaff auch Mare Crisium* in 1960, Schmidt announced that *Zettels Traum* would be written and photostatically reproduced with a text of *three* columns : a main middle one

---

(15) Cf. Hans-Michael Bock, " Potz Geck und kein Ende ! Arno Schmidt und die Presse ", in *Der Solipsist in der Heide. Materialien zum Werk Arno Schmidts,* ed. by Hans-Michael Bock and Jörg Drews, München 1974, p. 130-162.

(16) William York Tindall, *A Reader's Guide to 'Finnegans Wake',* London 1969, p. 24.

giving the " realistic " dialogue, observations and actions of the main characters during one day in the summer of 1968 in a small village in Northern Germany; a second column on the left with quotations from the works of Poe, who is the subject of most of the discussion going on in the text itself; a third column on the right side with the daydreams, " thought plays " (" Gedankenspiele "), reflections and memories of the hero and fictional narrator Daniel Pagenstecher, Schmidt's alter ego, as well as other quotations from a variety of poets (from Cooper to Goethe, Wieland to Joyce). " ...Not that I have the ambition to mix up as many plots and threads of narrative as possible... Joyce, in *Finnegans Wake* for instance, which actually is or at least should be a book in several columns, has taken the easy way out and has simply printed everything in a mixed up way; well, he was fond of mystifications. I do think differently about that problem; I do not want to complicate things for the reader arbitrarily, and that's why I have kept apart the three main columns of the text, so that the reader immediately knows where he is... " (17)

Schmidt maintains, then, that Joyce wantonly complicated things by not keeping apart the levels or channels of the text. Schmidt's contention is based of course on the premise that these different levels in *Finnegans Wake* could have been, and still can be, separated definitely and that the text divides into a basic plot and all the " added " meanings. This conception, doubtful as it is, explains Schmidt's stated intention to build a different structure and a visual presentation of *Zettels Traum.* In opposing certain features of *Finnegans Wake,* Schmidt argues as a " realist " who wants to keep the main figures of *his* book clearly discernible and wants them to keep their feet solidly on the ground, and who furthermore thinks it necessary to indicate, through the graphic design of the page, what is added to the basic " realistic " situation or where it turns into daydream, myth, hallucination and where learned quotations are brought to bear upon it.

The result of this procedure is that almost everywhere − with the exception of certain puns, allusions, and fragmentary quotations in the central column − we have at least some foothold. At least a superficial understanding of what is going on remains possible. Whereas constant interpretative deciphering is required in the reading of the Wake, a lot of simple reading, simple at least for the trained reader of Schmidt's previous works, facilitates progress in *Zettels Traum.* There *are* metamorphoses of characters too, there are points in which persons change into historical or mythological beings, especially in Book IV and VII, but such transformations always constitute short interludes that come to an end as soon as clearly discernible states in the daydreaming or in hallucinations of the characters stop. There is a fixed set of not quite fixed characters, fixed in time and place throughout most of the book.

Also, there is almost always a definite " I " that is the centre of narration, observation, thinking, remembering, quoting, and so on. In only a few sentences

---

(17) Arno Schmidt, " Panorama von 'Zettels Traum' ". Radio-broadcast in two parts. 29.4.1969 and 13.5.1969. Transcript, Hamburg 1969, p. 3.

do the characters change their meaning or are transformed or replaced. The dreamlike quality of the events in *Zettels Traum* cannot be compared to the degree in which *Finnegans Wake* seems to imitate dream states in all their characteristics.

The language of *Zettels Traum* most of the time remains on a realistic level too. There are of course lots of individual words and isolated sentences which, by the techniques of hybrid formation, puns and portmanteau coinings, allow of more than one meaning. But on the whole, the devices known from *Finnegans Wake* are exploited much less densely and consistently in *Zettels Traum*. Let me quote two examples. The title of Book IV of *Zettels Traum* is " Die Geste des grossen Pun ", which can be read as " The Jests of the Great Pan ", " The Guests of the Great Pan ", or "The Jests of the Great Pun " or else " The Deeds of the Great Pen [is] " – and so on.. Similarly, the title of Book VII, " The twilit of the Guts " can be understood as " The Twilight of the Gods " (" Götterdämmerung ") or as " The Toilet of the Guts " (18). But such ambivalent or amphibolic spelling in *Zettels Traum* is more peripheral than in *Finnegans Wake*. It is hard to say whether the reduced density of a system of " freudful mistakes " is really the result of the " realistic " intentions of the author who – for the reader's sake – didn't want to exaggerate the method, or whether this points to a lack of daring, a lack of skill or a lack of imagination. " One great part of every human existence is passed in a state which cannot be rendered sensible by the use of wideawake language, cutanddry grammar and goahead plot ", Joyce wrote in a letter (19). There is much more wideawake language, cutanddry grammar and goahead plot in *Zettels Traum,* and much of the reader's irritation is caused simply by the unorthodox spelling that somehow approaches phonetic transcription of colloquial German and dialects spoken by the characters. As Tony Phelan put it : " Schmidt's texts are much more limited in the degree of play they allow the word. For all his admiration, he stops short... of the complete freedom of *Finnegans Wake*. (20)

Though lexical deviance or semantic licence obstruct the fluent reading of *Zettels Traum* much less, the techniques that remind us of *Finnegans Wake* are scattered all over the text. Around 1960 Arno Schmidt revised his concept of language and learned a lot from Lewis Carroll, James Joyce and Sigmund Freud : in terms of the *Traumdeutung* and *Die Psychopathologie des Alltagslebens* there is condensation, displacement, compromise-formation, overdetermination and symbolic representation of all sorts of parapraxes on the verbal level and in the imagery. But he certainly exaggerates in his statement that great parts of *Zettels Traum* are written in " etyms " – that is what he calls the elements of the vocabulary of the unconscious, verbal roots or germs which, according to the " etym theory " extensively discussed in *Zettels Traum,* can be found in every

---

(18) Clearly also in deference to " cultic twalette " and " guttergloomering " (FW 344.12, 565.2).

(19) 24 November 1926, *Letters III,* p. 146.

(20) Tony Phelan, " Rationalist narrative in some works of Arno Schmidt ". In : *Occasional Papers in German Studies,* No. 2, University of Warwick 1972, p. 36.

author. These *etyms* (21) can also be artistically *constructed* and used for a language that is not " wideawake ", but has the multidimensionality of the language of dreams. Yet the offspring of these verbal nuclei or verbal radiations are rooted in the unconscious, i.e. words homophonous or homonymous to these " etyms ", are not so very numerous in the text of *Zettels Traum*.

In *Zettels Traum* there is neither the allegorical generality of the characters of *Finnegans Wake* (Schmidt is very self-centered in the choice of his heroes : they are always his own alter egos, including Daniel Pagenstecher), nor is there any remarkable theory of history or of time. The hero and narrator Daniel Pagenstecher is not in any sense an " Everybody ", but definitely an older writer and translator and scholar about 60, and never anything else except perhaps a model case for the demonstration of problems ageing writers may have. The merging of one character into another, the simultaneous identification of the actual with the historical, with the mythical, does not happen in *Zettels Traum*.

The " limitations of the spatio-temporal world " (22) remain firm in Schmidt's book, except for the daydreamlike " Walpurgis-Spuk " in Book IV and the hallucinatory passages in the sexual phantasms in Book VII where a fun-fair is presented that is at the same time an encyclopaedia of sexual perversions. The identity of Daniel Pagenstecher might be doubted only in so far as he borders, as already mentioned, on the character of the author himself, whose ego-ideal he is and out of whose literary notebooks and collections and quotations he continually draws all the material of memories in the book. Pagenstecher, to a remarkable degree, is a masque, a *persona,* of the author, in part identical with him, Schmidt's alter ego in a book that might be called a megalomaniac dream with sado-masochistic elements. But in general *Zettels Traum* attempts neither to create a universal myth nor to break down the barriers between national languages. If there is a dialectic relation, or rather an osmotic or metamorphotic process between historical and/or individual persons on one side and mythical persons on the other, as in *Finnegans Wake,* then it is reduced to a much smaller scale. The characters, the constellation in which they confront each other, their conflicts are all mirrored in literary quotations from works of the past, added into one or the other of the marginal columns in a way, or with a necessity, that we cannot as yet assess critically. There are, as far as we can see, traces of such mythical conceptions of the characters of the book in so far as literary quotations seem to function, or are probably intended to function, as mirrors or echoes of timeless, never changing, everlasting human conflicts, fates, predicaments. But Schmidt hasn't pushed this very far, and at present we cannot make out yet with what consistency he has given everyday life a quasi-mythical dimension by piling buildung supra buildung in quotations. What we can see is that many quotations do not merge with the narrative, but look like superficial adjunctions, unintegrated

---

(21) Compare the wellknown phrase " The abnihilisation of the etym " (FW 353.22).

(22) Anthony Burgess, *Here Comes Everybody,* London 1965, p. 188.

into the flow of the story or the discussions going on. They appear like learned footnotes, or rather side-notes, obsessively and endlessly accumulated and rather arbitrarily associated. There are various languages from which quotations are drawn, but they mostly *remain* quotations, that is, something that came to the narrator's mind but doesn't yield additional shades of meaning. German is the basic language of *Zettels Traum* to a much higher degree than *Finnegans Wake* is written in English, and there is no tendency towards a universal language.

So the unification of languages into one new artificial idioglossary is perhaps not Schmidt's intention; certainly it is not achieved. Not even the plasticity of the German language is exploited to its full extent. Schmidt's ambition, as can be seen from the mere bulk of his venture, went more in the direction of quantity : he wanted to write *the* Great and Big Book of our day, and he did it by cramming in so much − especially some theoretical debates about Edgar Allan Poe and his own " etym theory ", which of course did not lend itself to all the tricks and charms of double talk − into the novel that in the end the qualitative aspect came to be neglected. That is the language, which at times remains plain and unelaborate to a surprising degree. In cases of doubt it seems he preferred to add new elements rather than to weld them into the text. So the language of *Zettels Traum* is devoid of the *melos* and musicality of the *Wake,* and instead of the rhythmic flow of words we get a slow and sometimes very hard-edged alignment of − certainly brilliant − elements. An excessive use of punctuation marks, separating sentences and phrases, works against the formation of rhythmic patterns, for which reason hearing the text spoken aloud, so vital for *Finnegans Wake,* does not greatly add to the understanding of *Zettels Traum.* The visual and graphic appearance − from the tricolumnar arrangement to an intricate and subtle system of punctuation − is dominant and significant. *Finnegans Wake* may in part be called an auditory work, *Zettels Traum* is almost exclusively designed for eye-reading.

Homage to the genius of James Joyce extends from Schmidt's novel *Die Gelehrtenrepublik* up to *Zettels Traum :* we find a Joyce memorial on the utopian IRAS island in the year 2008; the *Essential James Joyce* accompanies the hero Karl Richter on his weekend trip in *Kaff und Mare Crisium;* Joyce also provides some *motti* for several chapters of Schmidt's psychoanalytical study of Karl May, the popular German author of adventure stories, *Sitara und der Weg dorthin* (1963), and, as Robert Wohlleben has suggested (23), *Caliban über Setebos* of 1964 can be read as a tribute to Joyce, founder and master of the techniques first used in that novel. But Joyce's influence, and Schmidt's rivalry perhaps, are most obvious in *Zettels Traum.*

The first page of *Zettels Traum* immediately reveals the source of the arrangement in three columns − not so much the Bible as printed in the 16th

---

(23) Robert Wohlleben, " Götter und Helden in Niedersachsen. Über das mythologische Substrat des Personals in 'Caliban über Setebos' ". In *Bargfelder Bote,* Lieferung 3/June 1973.

century (24) (for instance some Luther editions), but the layout of chapter 10 of *Finnegans Wake*. Schmidt acknowledges several works of Joyce through words, names and motifs. Take for instance the first words of the left column : " Anna Muh-Muh ! " reminds us of Anna Livia as well as the moocow in the opening of *A Portrait*. The isolated " king " which heads the middle column may allude to two sentences in *Finnegans Wake,* and so does " Noah " in the right column (cf. " aquaface " *Finnegans Wake* 3.14) (25). The first page of *Finnegans Wake* contains " sosie sesthers wroth "; *Finnegans Wake* introduces Susannah at least indirectly through " Achab + Zedecias ", the two elders who watched her in her bath − along with the theme of voyeurism of the *Wake*. Voyeurism as a perverse inclination that causes feelings of guilt looms large in *Zettels Traum* too, as the central sin of Daniel Pagenstecher and his friend Paul Jacobi.

Further down the left column we find, within a quotation taken from Poe, the river Nile, reinforcing the Liffey theme from *Finnegans Wake,* transformed here into a rivulet over which Pagenstecher is bending together with Franziska, daughter of his friend Paul. " Nile " combines an evocation of " riverrun " with the mention of *" eau de Nil "* in the " sirens " chapter of *Ulysses*. The " Sirens " allusion is continued into Franziska's blouse − " Bluse...satinisch ainzuschau'n " (a blouse, into which he can peer satanically). Clearly " satanisch " recalls that Miss Douce and Miss Kennedy " pawed their blouses, both of black satin " (U 258) and, who knows ?, perhaps Boylan's insight into " the cut of [the shopgirl's] blouse " in " Wandering Rocks " (*U* 228).

Having crisscrossed the first page of *Zettels Traum* in a rewarding search of allusions, let us make a big jump to the end. One quote, " dyed rags, pinned round a squaw " adds but a comma to a phrase lifted from " Proteus " (*U* 40). In his inner monologue, represented by the right column of the text, Daniel Pagenstecher is counting backwards from 20 to 0, just as at the end of chapter 10 of *Finnegans Wake* we find a count from " Aun " (one) to " Geg " (ten). Schmidt has often commented on that page (308) of *Finnegans Wake,* and especially its marginal drawings. Schmidt uses the same device at various points in *Zettels Traum*.

There is then really a plurability of possibilities concerning parallels and echoes on *Finnegans Wake* in *Zettels Traum* − a riche field for scholars to come.

Jörg DREWS

---

(24) Compare the new print of the 1545-edition of the Bible, published as " D. Martin Luther. Die gantze Heilige Schrift. Deudsch 1545 ", München 1972.

(25) Cf. *Bargfelder Bote,* Lieferung 2/January 1973.

Structure in " Dubliners "

The Life Chronology of Dubliners *

That *Dubliners* as a collection of stories is highly structured is clear. From the day in August, 1904, when Joyce completed the first story " The Sisters ", he knew – and wrote a friend – that it was to be a " series of [ten] epicleti " on " hemiplegia or paralysis " (*Letters,* I, 55). This dominant unifying theme was eventually matched to a life chronology in the arrangement of the stories so that by 1906 when Joyce completed the fourteen story version that he submitted to the English publisher, Grant Richards, its complex internal design made it unique. He described it to the publisher in a statement now famous.

> My intention was to write a chapter of the moral history of my country and I chose Dublin for the scene because that city seemed to me the centre of paralysis. I have...presented it...under four of its aspects : childhood, adolescence, maturity and public life. The stories are arranged in this order (*Letters,* II, 134).

The version did not include " The Dead ", which was added at a later date, was longer and as a short story more conventional in structure.

This 1906 version was marked by extraordinary symmetry in the four groups of tales. It consisted of an opening triad of stories dealing with three fatherless boys respectively, a quartet of tales dealing with adolescents in matching pairs, another such quartet of tales of individual mature men and women, and a final triad of stories picturing groups of people in public situations. Finally, characteristic of what was to become a lifetime practice, Joyce made the final story both in this version and the later one round out the book by recalling its opening.

Though all protagonists are different, the effect is that of a life between the characters and situations, and by adopting in the first eleven stories a deliberate chronology in which with one exception the protagonist, male or female, rich or

---

* This paper is a summary report of a fuller study eventually published by the *James Joyce Quarterly* (vol. 14, n° 4, Summer 1977).

poor, seems slightly older than the main character of the previous tale. It is this chronology that I wish to discuss, first to explain a seeming contradiction in Joyce's description of it and, second, to suggest that the chronology of the book as a whole is more complex than it first appears. There are, in fact, two chronologies.

A preliminary : the age pattern. Even cursory examination indicates Joyce went to great pains to distinguish the age differences. In the three stories of childhood, " The Sisters ", " An Encounter ", and " Araby ", no ages are given, but each young boy seems distinctly older than the preceding one in his speech patterns, psychological reactions and societal experiences. In the next eight stories the ages of all main characters are stated or suggested. In the stories of adolescence Eveline in the story of that name is " over nineteen "; Jimmy Doyle of " After the Race " is " about twenty-six ". Lenehan of " Two Gallants " is thirty and his friend, Corley, about the same age. Robert Doran of " The Boarding House " is " thirty-four or thirty-five ", but Polly Mooney is only nineteen, the age of Eveline. In the quartet dealing with mature life, Chandler of " A Little Cloud " is only thirty-two, but his friend, Gallaher, the successful returned journalist, looks and acts older. The age of Farrington of " Counterparts " is not given, but his heaviness, lumbering gait, and the fact he has five children indicate he is older. Maria of " Clay " is an old maid whose former nursery charges are now grown up and have children of their own; and Mr. Duffy of " A Painful Case " is an old bachelor who has an abortive romance with a " younger " woman who dies at forty-three.

As one examines this chronology, the ages of the characters in the second group, which Joyce called that of " adolescence ", seem strange, since they range from 19 to the early thirties. Clearly Joyce is not using the common quasi-legal definition of *adolescence* as extending from the age of puberty, twelve in a girl and fourteen in a boy, to the age of majority, normally twenty-one. He is, in fact, using throughout a classical category which he applied to his own life. Ellmann states that as Joyce passed thirty − a " portentous year " − he " liked to remind his friends, a little pedantically, that the Romans had made seventeen the dividing line between *pueritia* [boyhood] and *adulescentia* [adolescence], and thirty-one the beginning of *iuventus* [young manhood or prime of life]. Joyce's groups follow this scheme basically. Throughout, the eleven stories of this chronology represent virtually a set of case histories of psychological and moral paralysis.

The final point I wish to make is that *Dubliners* presents not only this main chronology, which ends with the eleventh story, but also a second one that starts later and runs to the end of the book. It begins precisely at the middle of *Dubliners,* with the tales of mature life, and presents children who are successively older in the last seven stories and whose situation develops a second Joycean theme : " Ireland is the old sow that eats her farrow " (*Portrait,* p. 203). Paralyzed parents destroy their children. In these stories, the state chosen by the first generation will become the fate of the second. To illustrate : in " A Little Cloud ", the would-be poet Little Chandler learns through an epiphany involving his infant son that he is a " little man " who has irrevocably chosen a " little house ", a " little wife " and a little life. His wife, rejecting him, turns toward the baby whose own future is forecast in her words, " My little mannie ! My little mannie ! " In the companion story " Counterparts " the repetitive experiences of frustration and humiliation, of being beaten in various ways, that Farrington undergoes in the office and bars find their counterpart in his vicious beating of his " little boy ". Brutality breeds brutality. In " Clay " the children at the family Halloween party that Maria attends are somewhat older; and they include " two big girls " from next door. They play saucers, a fortune-telling game. Maria, the pathetic little spinster, chooses the clay, signifying death – a fate the family conceals from her. It is not the ring of marriage for which she longs. But the choices of the children are also significant. " One got the prayer-book [life as a nun], the other three got the water " [continued life] and only one the ring. The choices here represent the historical fate of Ireland's women, a large proportion of whom never marry. At the opening of " A Painful Case ", Mrs. Sinico's daughter is a " young girl " seventeen : four years later her mother's death from an alcoholic accident leaves her alone and publicly disgraced – as earlier her mother had felt alone and privately disgraced by Mr. Duffy's rejection.

In the final group, the very fact that the stories deal with " public life " and present groups of people, makes this secondary theme of parents and children intrinsically more difficult to deal with. But it remains important. For example, " Ivy Day in the Committee Room " presents a contrast of generations : on the political level a contrast of Parnell and his followers; and on a more personal level a family contrast in the case of Old Jack, the caretaker, who complains that his nineteen year old son has become a booser. And we soon see *how :* – when they urge drink on a delivery boy who is only seventeen. " That's the way it begins ", said Old Jack. And another answers, " The thin edge of the wedge ". As fathers, so sons. In " A Mother ", Mrs. Kearney's frustration in not achieving " a brilliant life " in her marriage finds expression in her maneuvering her daughter Kathleen toward a concert career. But in the end her mercenariness overcomes her ambition when she orders her daughter out of a theatre rather than risk not being paid. The final words applied to the girl augur her fate : " Kathleen followed her mother meekly " – out to the same empty life. As mother, so daughter. Even in " Grace ", the final story of the 1906 version, which is a major attack on religiosity in Ireland, the theme is not absent. " Grace " deals with an alcoholic salesman, Tom Kernan, and the attempt by his friends to " intersect the arc of his... decline " by persuading him to make a retreat. His two older sons, reared in a more peaceable segment of the arc are well launched as merchants like their father, but it is otherwise with the three younger children. It is the discovery by a friend of their bad manners and accents, their rudeness and horseplay, that motivates the attempt at reformation. His wife, however, has few illusions about the possibility of improvement for the family.

Finally " The Dead ", written later and offering a restatement of all the major themes, includes this motif as a part of its thematic structure. For this story contrasts generations in a moribund society. The old Miss Morkans represent the culture of an outmoded and stereotyped generation that is dying. Their niece, Mary Jane, and nephew, Gabriel Conroy, represent Joyce's generation. Mary Jane is the final embodiment of Dublin's daughters in the book. Hailed at the party as one of the " Three Graces of the Dublin musical world ", she is a spinster, a provincial music teacher playing conventional airs. And Gabriel, the product of Dublin's intellectuality, is a frustrated school teacher and insecure husband. His great epiphany is the realization he has never really lived. This second chronological cycle thus ends where it began with men and women at the start of their mature life – apparently doomed to the living death of Dublin society.

Florence L. WALZL
University of Wisconsin

The chamber music of Molly and Alp and their ilk

The woman of Chamber Music

(Abstract)

The woman of *CM* must, like the scattered Osiris, be retrieved, piece by piece, from the wreckage of Joyce's own careful structure. Stanislaus arranged the individual poems in groups on the basis of content and mood. Joyce had constructed a movement from loneliness through courtship and consummation to disillusionment and loneliness. His woman emerges a clear Irish figure, lovely, graceful, shy, talented, passionate, affectionate, selfish, sensitive, possessive, intuitive, guilt-ridden, resentful, cold, determined — a woman of infinite variety. In his climactic song of consummation (XIV in Stanisłaus's ordering, a central 17 in Joyce's 34 poems) taken wholly from the Song of Songs, she has the Jewish beauty and passion of the Queen of Sheba, the mystery of Anastashie (*FW* 403). She has the glory of Mary the source of the human Word, the happy purity of Beatrice, the shy virginity of Stephen's Mercedes, Lady of Mercy. She has the taint of Jewish Zoe, sterile source of life, like the Dead Sea. She has the witchery of the villanelle's Temptress, of Circe, of Titania. She has the malice of the Vampire, seeking the poet's mouth like the Pale Vampire of *Ulysses*. She reveals the incomprehensible complexities of human love. She provides the springs of inspiration, the necessary insights into human hopes and fears confronting cosmic mysteries (like those expressed in " Kubla Khan " and *Macbeth*), which the poet cannot of himself experience. This woman of Joyce's youth, in spite of the flaws which adolescent certitudes and artistic uncertainties left her with, still does all that a woman composed of ink can do to make defect perfection.

Robert BOYLE
Marquette University

Why is Milly in Mullingar ?

(Abstract)

In the library, Stephen, referring to Pericles, " tried like another Ulysses ", asks : " Will any man love the daughter if he has not loved the mother ? " (195). This allusion suggests a structure parallel to the plays in *Ulysses,* culminating in the abortive attempt by Bloom/Ulysses/Pericles to effect a *Pericles*-dénouement by bringing Stephen into his home as a suitor for Milly, (exiled like Marina at 14), which would have as its counterpart, Bloom's reconciliation with Molly.

I find much textual support throughout the novel for Milly's exile in Mullingar pointing to the incest that lies at the heart of the novel. June 16, 1904, is nine months and one day after her " consummation of puberty " (736). Stephen, " a judge of imposters ", alludes to three transgressions by Bloom who is " stained by the mire of an indelible dishonour ". These have occurred " once by inadvertence, twice by design " (692).

This evidence is supported in three ways : 1) By factual details concerning the Bloom/Milly relationship, usually divulged by an omniscient narrator, 2) by allusions to literary works or to situations in which the father/daughter/suitor triangle is a central theme : *King Lear,* Bellini's *La Sonnambula,* Mozart's *Don Giovanni,* and the later Shakespeare plays. The blind stripling is a Tiresias-figure whose reiterated cane-tapping echoes the incest-revelation motif in *Oedipus Rex.* These allusions and others, augmented by puns and double entendres, are in turn supported by a number of changes Joyce made by hand in the typescripts, which reinforce father/daughter implications made elsewhere.

Bloom's efforts to bring Stephen home are focused on " a permanent eventuality of reconciliatory union between a school-fellow and a Jew's daughter ", since " the way to daughter led through mother, the way to mother through daughter " (695). But Bloom's plans for a quadrilateral *Pericles*-reconciliation are frustrated by Stephen's departure.

Jane FORD

Gerty MacDowell : Nymph or Nun ?

One of the issues which we ought to consider in our discussion of " Joyce's Women Characters " is the critical debate over Gerty MacDowell. Is Gerty a nymph or a nun ? Is Joyce's portrait of the young woman sympathetic ? Or is it simply satirical and mocking ? Does Joyce want us to empathize with his starry-eyed Nausicaa ? Or is he using her to exorcise his own romantic sentimentality and to poke fun at a manipulative, commercially-minded society ?

Certainly Joyce's portrait of Gerty MacDowell provides an incisive critique of a female self-image controlled by the popular media. Gerty has been reared on sentimental journalese. Subjected to a daily bombardment by countless Cinderella ads, she has constructed a romantic world of impossible fantasy. Gerty pines for a Prince Charming to rescue her from the dullness of Dublin life. She feels convinced that if she makes use of all the products offered by Madame Verity and *Woman Beautiful,* she will surely attract the man of her dreams.

Joyce's parodic bourgeois heroine has been formed by the sticky romanticism that deluded an earlier literary figure, Emma Bovary. Her mind has been shaped by the clichéd rhetoric of feminine journalism. Gerty not only speaks, but *thinks,* in a " namby-pamby jammy marmalady drawersy style ". She has been seduced by commercial promises of instant panacea − by ads that promote a simpering obfuscation of reality. It is ironically appropriate that she should be attracted to Leopold Bloom, whose career as an ad canvasser depends on public gullibility. Commercial art deceives, manipulates, and ultimately paralyzes.

Caught in a trap of self-deception, Gerty MacDowell places naive faith in all the opiates her society has to offer : religion and poetry, *eyebrowleine* and romantic myth. She pathetically snatches at the least sign of interest or affection to fire her amorous dreams. Years ago at a children's party, Reggy Wylie " snatched a half kiss... but it was only the end of her nose " (*U* 351). This memory seems to be the principal treasure in Gerty's barren hope-chest. Like the Citizen in " Cyclops ", the young girl fosters an inflated perception of herself. She constructs " worlds " from words, gestures, a peck on the nose and a vacation post card.

Rejected by her child-lover, Gerty yearns for an older man who will offer her both passion and compassionate understanding. Like Stephen Dedalus, Gerty has been deserted by an alcoholic " consubstantial " progenitor and is in search of a surrogate father. God, Leopold Bloom, and Father Conroy all seem promising candidates. But Bloom, the dark stranger, best fits her dreams of a " beau ideal ". Gerty turns to Bloom for paternal solicitude : safe in the " sheltering arms " of her father-lover, she no longer need fear rejection for that " one shortcoming " (*U* 364). Intuitively, Gerty knows that no cosmetic will ever sufficiently compensate for her lameness or give her an equal chance on the marriage market. Physical deformity has cheated her of her amorous " birthright ".

Joyce tempts us to think of his Nausicaa as a virginal nymphette, a sweet young Lolita barely out of undies : " As for undies they were Gerty's chief care and who that knows the fluttering hopes and fears of sweet seventeen... " (*U* 350). But Gerty is no longer an adolescent. We are prepared to accept her as a starry-eyed teenager. Joyce teases us, then deflates our expectations by adding, " though Gerty would never see seventeen again " (*U* 350). She will be " twenty-two in November " (*U* 352), the same age as Stephen Dedalus. Gerty has reached her majority : she *should* be " womanly wise ", but is not. In Dublin of 1904, Gerty MacDowell is fast on the decline toward old maidenhood. Despite elaborate dreams of matrimony, she is still unkissed (or half so), unwedded, and unbedded. Occasionally the grouchy, vindictive spinster breaks through her romantic façade, and we get a glimpse of Gerty's true nature : " The exasperating little brats of twins began to quarrel again... Little monkeys common as ditchwater. Someone ought to take them and give them a good hiding for themselves to keep them in their places " (*U* 359).

With intermittent sadistic lapses, Gerty retreats into a spiritualized notion of herself and her beau ideal. Considering the paucity of her amorous experiences in the past, one can assume that June 16, 1904, will be a landmark in her imagination. She has proved, perhaps for the first time, that she can attract and arouse male sexual interest : " And while she gazed her heart went pitpat. Yes, it was her he was looking at and there was meaning in his look. His eyes burned into her " (*U* 357). Gerty's heightened emotion corresponds to Bloom's tumescence : the stranger spiritually seduces her and scorches her with his gaze.

Choir music from the Catholic benediction service provides a fitting background for her titillating striptease. As the music rises, so does Bloom; and so do Gerty's skirts. Her foot simulates the piston and cylinder movement of the sexual act, and the young seductress takes vicarious pleasure in Leopold's agitation. The two re-enact the primal temptation between Eve and the Serpent in the Garden of Eden : " He was eying her as a snake eyes its prey. Her woman's instinct told her that she had raised the devil in him " (*U* 360).

Gerty innocently blushes at the euphemistic reference to Bloom's erection. But she is less innocent than she will admit : " She knew about the passion of men like that, hot-blooded, because Bertha Supple told her once... about the gentleman lodger " (*U* 365). Nevertheless, she deliberately exposes herself and takes pleasure in Bloom's arousal. Good Catholic that she is, Gerty recognizes her " sin " and absolves herself in advance : " Besides there was absolution so long as you didn't do the other thing before being married... and besides it was on account of that other thing coming on " (*U* 366). With a voice sounding suspiciously like Molly Bloom's, Gerty argues that all sins can be forgiven in confession and that it's " only natural " to feel sexual desire at the time of menstruation.

Our heroine is determined to preserve her chastity and not to " do the other thing before getting married ". She has nothing but contempt for prostitutes and " fallen women ". Spiritual masturbation may be as close as Gerty ever comes to sexual expression. Beneath her romantic dreams of matrimony lies a virginal terror of sexuality : " No, no : not that. They would be just good friends like a big brother and sister without all that other... " (*U* 364).

Leopold Bloom has proved to be Gerty's ideal," her all in all, the only man in the world for her for love was the master guide " (*U* 365). Bloom assures the young woman of her attraction, but he makes no physical demands. He " knows what a woman is " and respects the privacy of her solipsistic dream-world. Leopold is the perfect " Platonic " lover : like a chaste courtier, he pierces his lady with nothing more dangerous than a burning gaze.

Suzette A. HENKE
Charlottesville, Virginia

Molly as a Conventional Character

(Abstract)

Molly Bloom's characteristics are one-sidedly " feminine ". While Molly's conradictoriness in her monologue is amusing, and while some critics find it " intriguing ", Joyce bases his comedy on the assumption that the way a woman thinks is irrational and disconnected. Molly's dreams of a romantic life and her preoccupation with sex are as much a part of traditional convention as the fact that she is a sex object. She remains frustrated in her sex life and in her passive existence, the domineering tone and manipulative actions being signs of this frustration, not of strength or mastery. In the last two pages of her monologue, Molly does not transcend the dullness of her life by having an epiphany. Transformed from a conventional figure to a symbol, she remains dehumanized, amoral. The character of Molly Bloom on the realistic level is composed of traditionally weak " feminine " traits. Those strong characteristics often associated with women − kindness, tolerance, parental love − Molly lacks. Therefore, the reader might ridicule and pity Molly but finds it difficult to empathize with her.

Elaine UNKELESS
Cambridge,Mass

Molly's Rivals, Fanny M'Coy
and Kathleen Kearney in Ulysses :
Two Vocalists from the Dubliners Stories

Of the thirty-three characters from the *Dubliners* stories who are carried into *Ulysses,* several were chosen because they act as foils for Molly Bloom. Molly's characterization offered Joyce some problems in that, except for her brief appearance in the " Calypso " episode and an even briefer one in " Wandering Rocks ", she does not appear again until the final chapter, " Penelope ". Certain aspects of her personality, notably her musical interests and her sexuality, needed earlier development, and Joyce gave fuller dimension to her character by contrasts with other women in the novel. He raided *Dubliners* for its wives of similar age and social class as Molly's and for its vocalists. Among the singers recalled in Bloom's consciousness and Molly's are notably the young balladeer Kathleen Kearney of " A Mother " and Molly's contemporary, Mrs Fanny M'Coy, the soprano mentioned as the wife of the coroner's assistant C. P. M'Coy in " Grace ".

Elaborate sets of double parallels are developed between the Blooms and the M'Coys in *Ulysses.* Both pairs have musical backgrounds. In " Grace " M'Coy is described as having been a " tenor of some repute " and his wife as a soprano forced to teach " young children to play the piano at low terms " (p. 158). In a checkered career not unlike Leopold Bloom's, M'Coy had been " driven to live by his wits " and recently has been engaged in a low " crusade in search of valises and port-manteaus to enable Mrs M'Coy to fulfil imaginary engagements in the country " (pp. 158 and 160). (The pawned luggage is never again seen by its owners). Throughout *Ulysses* both men are trying to use their wives' singing careers to advantage – but the contrasts redound to Bloom's side. For example, M'Coy's boast that his wife has " just got an engagement " though it's " not settled yet " is such an obvious fabrication that Bloom thinks " Valise tack again ". However, Bloom's rejoinder " my wife too... she's going to sing... in Ulster Hall, Belfast " is fact (p. 74).

The women are also made parallels in various ways. Mrs M'Coy, a " reedy freckled soprano " with a " cheeseparing nose " is contrasted to handsome, voluptuous Molly. Neither has had recent concert engagements. Molly worries that she hasn't had one since she sang in St. Teresa's Temperance Hall in Clarendon Street a year ago. As fictional technique, a rivalry of their voices and concert engagements becomes an important motif throughout *Ulysses.* Its main purport is to keep before the reader Molly's liaison with her concert manager, Blazes Boylan. Though Bloom disbelieves M'Coy, he recognizes his likeness to him as they exchange news about their wives, " You and me, don't you know : In the same boat. Softsoaping " (p. 75). As the women are contrasted in conversation and his thoughts all through the day he becomes more and more agitated − and it is evident his antagonism against the M'Coys is sublimation of his real rivalry with Boylan. From " Sirens " on Bloom's increasingly caustic comments on Mrs M'Coy's vocal equipment substitute for his feelings about Boylan. Hearing the minuet from *Don Giovanni* in the Ormond bar, he recalls a cuckoldry he cannot face and he masks it from himself by thinking " M'Coy valise. My wife and your wife. Squealing cat " (p. 277). In " Eumaeus ", the day nearly over, he decides he will promote a concert tour for Mally himself : " Not, of course, with a hole and scratch company or local ladies on the job, witness Mrs C. P. M'Coy type... No, something topnotch, an all star Irish cast, the Tweedy-Flower grand opera company... " (p. 611). He never mentions Boylan. He thus triumphs vicariously over the M'Coys. That this rivalry between Fanny M'Coy and Molly is not real becomes apparent in " Penelope ". Molly, who has a professional's jealousy of every other vocalist thinks only once of Mrs M'Coy. She dismisses her as no competition. She's a " white head of cabbage skinny thing with a turn in her eye trying to sing my songs shed want to be born all over again and her old green dress with the lowneck as she cant attract them any other way " (p. 758). So much for poor Fanny.

The rivalry Molly feels keenly involves a singer who is younger and better attuned to newer popular interests, especially the new nationalism. It is Kathleen Kearney who arouses Molly's intense resentment : " little chits of misses they have now singing ", " Kathleen Kearney and her lot of squealers Miss This and Miss That Miss Theother lot of sparrowfarts skitting around talking about politics they know as much about as my backside " (p. 748). It is a sobering thought to Molly that she probably got last year's engagement in St. Teresa's Temperance Hall largely on account of her father's " being in the army " and her willingness to sing Kipling's patriotic ballad, 'The Absent-Minded Beggar'. " However, she consoles herself in her rivalry with these " Irish homemade beauties " − " bootmakers and publicans " daughters on grounds other than musical. She reassures herself : " They never walked the Alameda on an officers arm " and she thinks " I knew more about men and life when I was 15 than theyll all know at 50 ". She thinks of " Love's Old Sweet Song " that she means to sing in Belfast. " They havent passion "; they " dont know how to sing a song like that ". No man can " look at my mouth and teeth smiling like that and not think of it... let them get a husband first thats fit to be looked at and a daughter like mine and... a swell with money... like Boylan... I could have been a prima donna " (pp. 762-763). So in the end for Molly, rivalry in music dissolves into triumph in amour.

Florence L. WALZL
University of Wisconsin-Milwaukee

L'eau et les rêves
dans « Anna Livia Plurabelle »

L'eau pour Melville, dans son introduction à *Moby Dick,* est l'élément même de la rêverie, l'image de la vie et de ses profondeurs :

« Let the most absent-minded of men be plunged in his deepest reveries – stand that man on his legs, set his feet agoing, and he will infallibly lead you to water, if water there be at all in that region. Should you ever be athirst in the great American desert, try this experiment, if your caravan happens to be supplied with a metaphysical professor. Yes, as every one knows, meditation and water are wedded for ever ». « And still deeper », dit-il un peu plus loin, « the meaning of that story of Narcissus, who because he could not grasp the tormenting mild image he saw in the fountain, plunged into it and was drowned. But that same image, we ourselves see in all rivers and oceans. It is the image of the ungraspable phantom of life; and this is the key to it all ».

Un type particulier d'imagination est lié à l'eau, selon Bachelard. L'eau est l'élément des métamorphoses, l'image concrète du mobilisme héraclitéen ; et le destin de l'homme, transitoire et toujours recommencé, est identique au destin de l'eau [1].

L'héroïne de *Finnegans Wake,* dès l'origine, est une rivière [2]. La symbolique de l'eau s'enrichit et s'approfondit à mesure que s'écrit l'épisode : un mythe se dessine peu à peu. Anna Livia Plurabelle correspond au grand principe féminin de l'univers. Dans la version finale, elle apparaît dès l'ouverture, avec les flots de la Liffey, et se jette dans l'océan aux dernières pages du livre. Le cours entier des âges et des mythes tient dans son cycle toujours recommencé, de la source à l'océan, de l'océan à la source. L'épisode qui la célèbre constitue un reflet et un centre, le microcosme du livre tout entier.

Les irlandais de la Renaissance Celtique étaient très occupés de symboles, de correspondances, d'ésotérismes ; et le symbolisme de l'eau est un des éléments

---

(1) Voir Gaston Bachelard, L'Eau et les rêves, Paris, José Corti, 1942, Introduction.

(2) La Liffey est en vérité un petit fleuve ; l'anglais ne fait pas la distinction. Notre choix est déterminé par les impératifs de la langue française, et surtout par les caractères symboliques qui sont, pour l'essentiel, ceux de la rivière.

dominants de la poésie de Yeats. Mais c'est chez Jung, sans aucun doute, que Joyce a trouvé l'essentiel de son inspiration, avec un sentiment cosmique des éléments qui s'accorde à son imagination. Frazer, souvent évoqué à propos des sources symboliques de Joyce, ne mentionne dans *The Golden Bough* que les rites des faiseurs de pluie. Bachelard que Joyce n'a pu lire et qui semble, pour sa part, ignorer Joyce, a souvent les mêmes accents que lui pour décrire l'eau et la rivière. *L'Eau et les rêves* (3), de façon paradoxale, est peut-être la meilleure exégèse d'« Anna Livia Plurabelle ».

A la fois femme et rivière, Anna Livia est la nymphe de la Liffey, légère et dansante, claire et joyeuse que Joyce n'évoque jamais sans tendresse. Dans la symbolique universelle de l'eau, il puise les éléments qui composeront son héroïne. Toute différente de l'image traditionnelle, usée, purement visuelle, inspirée d'une antiquité de convention et coupée de ses racines profondes la naïade joycienne participe d'un symbolisme originel, organique, authentiquement onirique, comme il convient à un livre dont le domaine est l'inconscient.

Dès les premières esquisses de l'épisode la fusion est totale entre la femme et la rivière. Joyce parvient à établir un équilibre entre le particulier et l'universel, la réalité humaine et la nature. Son héroïne a la chevelure et le prénom de Livia Schmitz, la femme de son ami Italo Svevo, et le style de l'épisode évoque souvent le bavardage des lettres de Nora Joyce et des monologues de Molly Bloom. La Liffey elle-même est précisément caractérisée par son cours et les paysages qu'elle traverse.

La figure féminine s'identifie étroitement à la Liffey ; le lit, les rives l'embouchure de la rivière, correspondent clairement au corps de la femme dans la chanson d'Anna Livia.

Quant à l'histoire des amours enfantines d'Anna, c'est l'histoire de la rivière depuis sa naissance, mince filet d'eau qui s'échappe de sa source, petite fille qui échappe à sa nourrice. Elle attire à elle les ruisseaux et leur apprend ses danses et ses chansons, et Anna, telle une maquerelle, attire chez elle les servantes pour leur apprendre un nouveau métier. Tout terme de comparaison est écarté, et la notion même de métaphore est inconciliable avec cette fusion parfaite de deux réalités. Le paysage qui sert de décor aux amours d'Anna est celui où coule la rivière, depuis sa source dans les Monts de Wicklow, sa traversée du Comté de Kildare, où sa chevelure prend la couleur rousse des tourbières, et des champs d'orge du Comté de Dublin. Les caprices d'Anna, ses impertinences et ses chansons appartiennent à l'eau de la Liffey. Joyce évoque Anna Livia à sa toilette, figure gracieuse et fantastique, la chevelure ornée d'herbes aquatiques et de roseaux, parée de bracelets de cailloux et de galets. La grâce de cette évocation n'exclut pas l'humour. Ses boucles d'oreilles sont des pelures de pommes de terre, légume

---

(3) Gaston Bachelard, *L'Eau et les rêves, Essai sur l'imagination* de la matière, Paris, Librairie José Corti, 1942. Voir aussi J. Genêt « la poétique de l'eau chez W.B. Yeats », in *Actes du Congrès de Grenoble* (1973), S.A.E.S., Paris, Didier, 1976.

irlandais par excellence, elle porte sur le nez une pince à linge (4), et la traîne de sa robe brune s'étend derrière elle sur cinquante miles (5).

Figure vivante et familière, Anna Livia est aussi un mythe universel. Molly Bloom était avec moins d'évidence la terre, ou le double parodique de Pénélope.

L'eau, la rivière, l'élément féminin, se confondent et s'expriment mutuellement. Symbole féminin, l'eau s'incarne dans la figure d'Anna. La souplesse de la construction du texte, avec ses retours en arrière, ses interruptions, ses reprises, les métamorphoses perpétuelles d'Anna, la fraîcheur et la fantaisie de l'évocation, correspondent à tout ce que l'être a de mobile et de féminin. Joyce, dès la première version, semble démontrer cette continuité entre la parole de l'eau et la parole humaine que décèle Bachelard (6) : car c'est bien l'eau qui parle à travers le dialogue des lavandières, et le rythme rapide de la prose poétique a déjà cette fluidité qui caractérise la syntaxe de l'eau. Les consonnes liquides sont fréquentes, en particulier dans les premières phrases qui reviennent comme un leitmotiv ; et le nom de l'héroïne, si souvent prononcé, semble donner à Bachelard, qui remarque, après Bachoffen, que la voyelle A est la voyelle de l'eau (7).

L'eau de la rivière reflète le monde, et Anna Livia à sa toilette n'a pas de miroir, du moins dans les premières versions. L'eau est le miroir de l'Irlande, les tourbières et les ajoncs, les champs d'orge et de pommes de terre s'y reflètent. La rivière se confond avec le paysage qu'elle traverse et lui donne la conscience de sa beauté ; le charme et la fantaisie d'Anna Livia se communiquent au monde. L'imagination créatrice de Joyce s'identifie au rêve de l'eau, à ses reflets, à ses métamorphoses. Son expérience poétique dépend étroitement d'une expérience onirique. La figure d'Anna Livia est l'expression parfaite de cette union pancaliste du visible et de la vision dont Bachelard fait une loi élémentaire de l'imagination et de ce qu'il appelle le narcissisme cosmique (8).

Le caractère féminin d'Anna est nettement marqué, et non seulement par sa longue chevelure de naïade. Joyce en fait une coquette, une amoureuse, une entremetteuse, et, sans doute inspiré par Freud, évoque sa sexualité enfantine. Yeats, qui se plaisait, comme ses amis occultistes, à découvrir des réseaux de correspondances dans l'univers, associe à l'eau le sang, les organes sexuels et la passion (9). Jung retrouve dans les symboles alchimiques une identification de l'eau à son contraire, le feu (10). Pour lui, la source représente la chaleur de la vie, son ardeur, le secret de la passion ; elle est liée au monde des instincts (11).

---

(4) C'est là sans doute une allusion à un pont métallique sur la Liffey qui défigure Dublin.

(5) C'est la longueur de la Liffey.

(6) *L'Eau et les rêves*, p. 22.

(7) Ibid., p. 253.

(8) Ibid., p. 40-45.

(9) Lettre à Olivia Shakespear du 24 juillet 1934. *Letters* p. 823-824.

(10) C.G. Jung, *Psychologie et Alchimie* Trad. Pernet et Cahen, Paris, Buchet/Chastel, 1970, p. 305.

(11) Ibid., p. 159.

L'eau est traditionnellement associée à la vie. Source de vie, elle symbolise l'origine de la création : les eaux primordiales contiennent toutes les promesses, l'infini des possibles. Frazer évoque l'eau de vie à propos des mythes babyloniens (12), et Jung fait de la figure maternelle la source de l'eau vitale (13). L'eau symbolise la fertilité, et Anna Livia, comme la Cybèle de Frazer (14), est une sorte de déesse mère à la fécondité inépuisable. Dès la première version, elle a 111 enfants. C'est le chiffre cent qui symbolise le plus couramment la multitude et la totalité. Le chiffre onze est lié aux mystères de la fécondité, et de l'excès, de la démesure; pour Saint Augustin « le nombre onze est l'armoirie du péché » (15). Le vieillard des eaux, dans la légende russe, a comme Anna cent onze enfants, dont le nombre symbolise la plénitude (16).

L'eau douce est pour Bachelard la véritable eau mythique. Symbole universel et ambivalent, elle résoud les antinomies. La rivière représente traditionnellement le cours de la vie et le flux du temps : elle sera dans *Finnegans Wake* un principe d'unité.

Dès le *Portrait,* l'eau constituait un thème symbolique ambivalent, lié au développement de Stephen. Froide, bourbeuse, sombre, stagnante, ou tumultueuse ou menaçante au début du livre, elle est dans ses derniers chapitres associée à la joie, à la liberté, à la création, et préside à la seconde naissance de Stephen. Dans *Finnegans Wake* elle est aussi, et de façon plus marquée, un élément ambivalent, lié à la fois à la création et à la dissolution, symbole de vie et de mort. Anna Livia est ici d'une jeunesse qui semble éternelle; en dépit de ses innombrables enfants, elle semble avoir dix ans. Force féconde et rénovatrice, l'eau de jouvence rafraîchit et rajeunit; l'eau provoque aussi, par le bain lustral ou le baptême, la renaissance spirituelle; elle symbolise la vitalité de l'être psychique. Matière primordiale, source de toutes choses, elle manifeste le transcendant, et ouvre l'accès à l'éternité. L'eau apparaîtra, dans la suite du livre, comme une substance mortelle, mais qui fait vivre par delà la mort; le sac d'Anna Livia, mentionné deux fois dans le texte A, symbolisera cette fonction. Dans *Finnegans Wake* l'élément liquide joue le rôle de médiateur entre la vie et la mort. Il est à la fois le flux du temps qui passe et conduit à la mort, et une présence immuable, symbole d'éternité. La rivière résoud l'opposition du devenir et de la continuité. C'est par excellence le lieu poétique du cycle de la naissance, de la mort et de la renaissance, de cet éternel retour présent dans la structure même du livre. Les cycles répétés de la rivière correspondront aux cycles de l'histoire.

Image de l'âme individuelle et universelle, l'eau symbolise la mémoire et l'inconscient; Jung y voyait une représentation de l'inconscient collectif. Paysage

---

(12) *The Golden Bough,* p. 326.

(13) *Psychologie et Alchimie,* p. 97.

(14) *The Golden Bough,* p. 353.

(15) Dictionnaire des symboles, Paris, Seghers, 2ᵉ édition, 1974, p. 321-322.

(16) Joseph Campbell and Henry Morton Robinson, *A Skeleton Key to Finnegans Wake,* 1944; Viking Compas édition, New York, 1961, p. 135.

de rêve et lieu des métamorphoses, l'eau est cette âme universelle, l'*anima mundi* qui conserve l'empreinte de toute l'expérience humaine. Joyce, dès la première version d'« Anna Livia Plurabelle », utilise d'une façon personnelle une symbolique universelle pour créer une figure mythique originale. La complexité symbolique de la rivière s'approfondira dans les versions successives de l'épisode. Les images nées de l'eau s'accordent, dès la première version, pour créer l'héroïne idéale d'une histoire onirique de l'univers.

La rêverie de Joyce est dirigée et contrôlée, mais profonde et naturelle. La même sincérité organique se retrouve chez Joyce et Claudel dans le sentiment du caractère matériel et dynamique de l'eau, élément lié au corps humain. Ces racines organiques de l'imagination, cette physiologie de l'eau onirique, nous les retrouvons dans la chanson d'Anna Livia, dans certaines images d'Edgar Poe, élucidées par Marie Bonaparte, et chez Claudel, dans une ode où le poète s'identifie aux fleuves, comme Anna Livia aux rivières :

> « Connaissant ma propre quantité,
> C'est moi, je tire, j'appelle sur toutes mes racines, le Gange, le Mississipi,
> L'épaisse touffe de l'Orénoque, le long fil du Rhin, le Nil avec sa double vessie... (17)

L'imagination organique se prolonge par une rêverie littéraire. Tous les complexes de culture, liés aux complexes originels et définis par Bachelard, le complexe de Caron, et celui d'Ophélie, de Narcisse, de Nausicaa, de Léda, sont présents dans « Anna Livia Plurabelle », avec d'autres, innombrables, ceux d'Isis, de Pandore ou d'Artémis.

L'épisode tout entier est l'illustration idéale de la théorie bachelardienne de la rêverie littéraire : ...« étrange rêverie, qui s'écrit, qui se coordonne en s'écrivant, qui dépasse systématiquement son rêve initial, mais qui reste quand même fidèle à des réalités oniriques élémentaires » (18).

Claude JACQUET
Université Paris III

(This text has been left in French, the language in which it was presented).

---

(17) Paul Claudel, *Cinq grandes Odes,* cité par Bachelard, *L'Eau et les rêves,* p. 13.

(18) Op. cit., p. 27.

Other panels

Textual and Editorial Problems, Chairman : Hans Walter Gabler, University of Münich; Philip Gaskell, Trinity College, Cambridge; Michael Groden, Princeton University; Walton Litz, Princeton University; John MacNicholas, university of South Carlina; Giorgio Melchiori, university of Rome.

Joyce, Eisenstein and Rutmann : Notions of Cinema, Chairman : Ruth Perlmutter, Institute of Cinema, Philadelphia; Sheldon Brivic, Temple University; James Naremore, University of Indiana; Léon Robel, France; Fred Haines.

Work since the « Wake », Chairman : David Hayman, University of Wisconsin; Philippe Sollers, *Tel Quel*; Maurice Roche.

The Shape and direction of « Ulysses » Scholarship, Chairman : T.F. Staley, University of Tulsa; Guido Almansi, School of English and American Studies, Norwich; Arnold Goldman, University of Sussex; Maurice Beebe, Temple University; William Schutte, Lawrence University.

Shakespeare and Joyce, Leslie Fiedler, State University of New York at Buffalo.

Foreign Languages in « Finnegans Wake », Chairman : Fritz Senn, Zürich; Marian Cumpiano, University of Puerto Rico; Rosa Maria Bosinelli, University of Bologna; Luigi Schenoni, Bologna; Nino Frank, Paris.

New Approaches to Joyce, Chairman, Robert A. Day, City University of New York; Walton Litz, Princeton University; Khachig Tölölyan, Wesleyan University; Diane Tolomeo, Victoria University.

Events

In addition to the panel discussions, the following Joyce-related events were programmed during the intermissions :

Joyce-ends : a « re-call », by Kathleen Bernard.

In Dublin's Quare City : a sketch by Basil Payne.

James Joyce's Paris : a personally introduced showing by Gisèle Freund of her film portraits from the 1920-1940 Parisian literary scene.

Molly Bloom : by the French actress « Garance », at the Récamier theatre, whose director, Antoine Bourseiller, invited Symposium participants to be his guests.

Anna Livia's awake : by Jean-Yves Bosseur. An original tape produced in collaboration with the *Atelier de Création Radiophonique de Radio-France.* Voices : Kathleen Bernard, Mary French, François Koklaere, Frank Mc Dermott, Lorna Monaghan, Henry Pillsbury, Niall O'Shea, Philippe Torrens.

Richard et Bertha, montage-démontage d'un couple : a montage based on *Exilés,* produced by Henry Pillsbury with Nadia Taleb (narrator), Madeleine Vim (Bertha), Jacques Baillon (Richard).

A text by Michel Butor, written for the occasion, served as basis for an audio-visual montage presented by the audio-visual services of the *Centre National d'Art et de Culture Georges Pompidou,* and produced by Fédor Ballo.

A background of Joycean sound effects : played from tapes produced by Jean-Yves Bosseur.

Table of contents

	Pages
Acknowledgements	5
« I write », *said Joyce*, Maria Jolas	7
« Circe » : Why, What and How, Chairman : Zack Bowen	11
The Paris Background of « Finnegans Wake », Chairman : J.S. Atherton.	27
Joyce and Politics, Richard Ellmann	31
Narrative in « Ulysses », Chairman : Shari Benstock	33
« A Portrait of the artist », Structure and Theme, Chairman : Margaret Church	59
The Non-Age of Joyce, Chairman : Morton Levitt	63
Joyce and Brancusi, Nathan Halper, Sidney Geist	69
Joyce's Corpus as Word-Machine, Chairman : Margaret Solomon	79
Joyce's Sly Rhetoric, Chairman : J. Mitchell Morse	93
Political Perspectives on Joyce's Work, Chairman : Morris Beja	101
Joyce and the Other Arts, Chairman : Archie Loss	125
Joyce's Influence on Arno Schmidt, Jörg Drews	133
Structure in « Dubliners », Florence L. Walzl	143
The Chamber Music of Molly and ALP and their ilk, Chairman : Robert Boyle	147

Table of contents, Volume I

	Pages
Présentation	5
Séance inaugurale à la Sorbonne	
'J'écris' dit Joyce, Maria Jolas	9
Joyce le Symptôme, Docteur J. Lacan	13
Le change du sens et le ça des mots, Collectif Change, avec J.P. Faye, Mitsou Ronat, Jacques Roubaud	19
Accueils français à Joyce entre les deux guerres, table ronde présidée par A. Anglès, avec la participation de Nino Frank, Jérôme Gillet, Maria Jolas, Patrick McCarthy, Georges Raillard et Philippe Soupault	37
Joyce et l'aventure d'aujourd'hui, table ronde présidée par Michel Butor, avec François Aubral, Jean-Yves Bosseur, Jean-Claude Montel, Nathalie Sarraute, Philippe Sollers	59
Anna Livia's Awake, Jean-Yves Bosseur	95
Joyce re-surrexité par Van Laere, Bruno Thiry	109
Catalogue de l'exposition « James Joyce et Paris », Bernard Gheerbrant	115

IMPRIMERIE LOUIS-JEAN
Publications scientifiques et littéraires
TYPO OFFSET

05002 GAP - Telephone 51 35 23 -

Dépôt légal 282-1979